# The
# ABC's
# of Behavior
# Change

by Frank J. Sparzo

Phi Delta Kappa Educational Foundation
Bloomington, Indiana U.S.A.

Cover design by
Victoria Voelker

Phi Delta Kappa Educational Foundation
408 North Union Street
Post Office Box 789
Bloomington, Indiana 47402-0789
U.S.A.

Printed in the United States of America

For Rosalie

# Table of Contents

# Preface

Fourteen years ago I published *Changing Behavior: A Practical Guide for Teachers and Parents*, which was number 221 in the well-known Phi Delta Kappa fastback series. Over the years, a number of teachers, parents, and students have suggested that I update and expand that publication. I am most grateful to the Phi Delta Kappa Educational Foundation for the opportunity to do so.

If learning can be defined as a change in behavior as a result of experience, then a book about changing behavior is a book about teaching and learning. When a teacher successfully shows a student how to set up an experiment, the teacher is providing the experience necessary for learning and the student is changing his or her behavior as a result of that experience. The same may be said about a parent who teaches a child to say "please," to tie a knot, or to share toys.

Just about everyone is involved in behavior change in one form or another. For example, corporations influence workers by offering raises and promotions for good performance, and they influence customers by pleasing them so that they will return. Similarly, therapists encourage changes in personality (detected by noting changes in verbal and nonverbal, public and private behaviors), while politicians influence voters by the promises they make. Even infants alter what others do: They cry until someone picks them up. Thus the subject matter of this little book goes far beyond a simple interest in changing this or that specific behavior. Its principles relate to a very broad range of human interactions, as well as a very broad range of circumstances.

The approach to changing behavior outlined in these pages is called behavior analysis. It does not focus on the traditional psychological terms that educators often use; there is no attempt to diagnose children for maladjustment or poor self-concept or any of the myriad other terms we use to refer to a person's feelings or

1

interior state. Instead, the focus is on the behavior itself and on the environmental circumstances that surround it.

For example, I once observed a disruptive elementary class in which students were off task about one-third the time. After the students left at the end of the day, I asked the teacher what she thought caused the problem. Without hesitation, she said, "They're maladjusted." Maladjustment, you can imagine, is a difficult problem for a single teacher to fix. So rather than search for "maladjustment," we did an ABC analysis to find out what classroom influences were at work. Then we designed a plan to encourage achievement. The plan did reduce student disruption.

That two-phase process, doing an ABC analysis and designing a plan, is what this book is all about.

I would like to thank Rosalie A. Rohm, Ph.D., R.N., and John K. Sparzo, M.D., who read the entire manuscript and offered a number of suggestions for improvement. I am grateful for their help. I also wish to thank Donovan Walling and David Ruetschlin for their skillful editing.

Frank J. Sparzo
Ball State University
Muncie, Indiana

# Chapter One

# Perspectives and Assumptions

Several years ago a teacher and former student, Sandra, came to my office concerned about a seven-year-old female who on occasion engaged in inappropriate sexual behavior in her classroom. This had been going on for several months. Early in our conversation she said, "I think the child has a poor self-concept." After hearing a number of details, I suggested a plan that involved minor changes in the classroom. Fortunately, the plan worked without a hitch. The child was easily taught to do other things.

Sandra's visit disturbed me for weeks. I wondered what former students *failed to learn* in my courses and in their methods classes. Sandra had a degree in education, had been teaching three years at the time of her visit, and was genuinely puzzled by what turned out to be a rather simple problem to solve. And I was partly responsible. I and others had failed to teach her practical ways to deal with a variety of problem behaviors. The fundamental difficulty appeared to be the way in which Sandra perceived the problem — in where she had learned to look for an explanation of behavior. Why had she overlooked the very problem she needed to confront?

Many people, like Sandra, seek to explain behavior by focusing on factors thought to reside in some way *within* the person. When attempting to explain behavior, they use such terms as attitude, value, habit, motive, personality, attention deficit, and so on. Sandra appeared to be partial to self-concept.

There are hundreds of terms that refer to feelings or inner states that presumably account for our actions. Many of these words and phrases are used freely by all of us in casual conversation; but when it comes to understanding behavior, they often let us down. How many times have we been invited to excuse or allow certain actions because the person has a "poor self-concept" or an "oppositional defiant disorder"? Such labels can paralyze us if we are not careful; after all, not much can be done when problems spring from within the person.

A vivid example comes to mind. A number of years ago a 17-year-old student, who had suffered serious neurological damage in an auto accident 20 months earlier, enrolled in a boarding school where I was an administrator. Although he had been a very good public school student and athlete prior to the accident, his initial months with us were very difficult ones. Now he was a discipline problem (once he held the headmaster at bay with a chair), and his academic progress was barely measurable. However, things improved dramatically as we became aware of our own problem: We had tried to explain what the student did and did not do by referring to his "neurological impairment." In effect, the label had paralyzed us; we were acting as though the student could no longer learn. We decided to make a concerted effort to provide feedback and consequences for his actions whenever we could. Subsequently, we learned that, yes, he learned more slowly now; yes, he did not learn as much as in the past; yes, he could learn to control himself. And yes, he eventually graduated.

Behavior analysts attempt to understand everyday behavior by focusing on the act itself and on the situational events that surround it. That is a much different perspective than most people take. For example, consider the situation of an 18-year-old female named Jill. On several occasions Jill bought clothes for herself and charged them to her parents' account. Her parents found out about Jill's shopping only when a new balance statement arrived or after Jill wore her new things. They scolded Jill, but without apparent effect. When asked for an explanation of her daughter's behavior, Jill's mother spoke of Jill's "uncaring attitude toward the family" and her "irresponsibility." Note that this explanation focuses on two assumed inner factors.

A behavior analyst would focus on the circumstances and the act of shopping. For example, as an indication of the seriousness of the behavior, he might simply try to determine how many times Jill charged the account in the past (two times could well be less of a problem than 10 would be). The analyst then would look for pertinent relationships between Jill's shopping and situational factors, especially those antecedents and consequences that accompany the act of shopping.

The circumstances that are present before shopping — the *antecedent* conditions — are important. It might be found, for instance, that Jill is especially likely to buy clothes when she has a date with a new boyfriend or that Jill's best girlfriend encourages her shopping. Certain *consequences* also influence Jill. For instance, she may attract compliments when she wears new clothing. She also may like what she sees when she models purchases in front of a mirror. And, if she likes the way the new clothes feel, tactile consequences are in play. The fact that Jill's parents, contrary to their complaints, ultimately paid for her purchases is another consequence that might account for Jill's actions.

Let us now compare the two viewpoints again. Like Sandra, Jill's mother turned to inner factors to explain her daughter's surreptitious shopping. In contrast, the behavior analyst focused on clothes-buying itself (its amount), on antecedents (when it occurred and with whom), and on consequences following the purchases (attention, visual and tactile stimulation, and parents' payment). This perspective did not rely on ambiguous explanations but on observable actions and their link with environmental events. Teachers and parents are in a relatively good position to make these kinds of observations.

## Assumptions

Eight assumptions and implications are relevant to the approach used in this book.

1. Most human behavior is largely learned. Although many behaviors are unlearned and a product of biological evolution (for

example, shivering in low temperatures), human behavior is broadly changeable and adaptable.

*Implication*: In learning, the consequences of behavior are often more important than are genetic predispositions. To change behavior, change the consequences.

2. People learn according to the same general principles of behavior, though some learn more quickly and easily than others.

*Implication*: Effective teaching and learning often require an individualized plan of action.

3. The general principles apply to undesirable as well as desirable behaviors.

*Implication*: People will learn undesirable or desirable behavior depending on the consequences that follow either kind of behavior. For example, those rewarded for dishonesty will learn to be dishonest; those rewarded for telling the truth will learn to tell the truth. As James Q. Wilson explained about teaching morality:

> children do not learn morality by learning maxims or clarifying values. They enhance their natural sentiments by being regularly induced by families, friends, and institutions to behave in accord with the most obvious standards of right conduct — fair dealing, reasonable self-control, and personal honesty. A moral life is perfected by practice more than by precept; children are not taught so much as habituated. In this sense schools inevitably teach morality. . . by such behavior as they reward and punish.*

4. Many behaviors occur only in specific settings.

*Implication*: It is important to identify specific situations that encourage desirable and undesirable behavior — students may behave badly in algebra but not in other classes; a child may cause trouble when he is with his mother but not when he is with his father.

*James Q. Wilson, *The Moral Sense* (New York: Free Press Paperback, 1997), p. 249.

5. Basic patterns of interacting with the world are learned early in life.

*Implication*: Intervene as early as possible, before problems become acute.

6. Long-standing behaviors may require persistent effort to change them.

*Implication*: Some behaviors have been rewarded hundreds of times (or more) and endure for that reason. When improvement in such cases is sluggish, be wary of abandoning a good plan of action too soon.

7. Neither excessive permissiveness nor authoritarianism has a glorious history of success in changing behavior.

*Implication*: Use the principles and procedures described in this book as consistently and humanely as possible.

8. The principles of behavior change — because they relate to such a wide range of human action — may at times seem quite simple. But sometimes knowledge of the principles is not enough.

*Implication*: Some problems are so serious — for example, delinquency, prolonged depression or anxiety, aggression toward self and others, autism, withdrawal, and drug addiction — as to require help by professionals who specialize in changing behavior.

## What Follows

Up to this point I have used an anecdote to illustrate a model of behavior without naming the model. It is called the ABC model of behavior, where A refers to *antecedent events* (A events) that occasion or cue behavior, B refers to the *behavior* itself, and C refers to *consequent events* (C events) that increase or decrease the likelihood of behavior. In Jill's case, attention was a plausible consequence (C) that made shopping (B) more likely on the occasion of an upcoming date (A). Chapter Two explores the practical aspects of the model in greater detail.

Chapter Three focuses on five kinds of consequences that shape behavior. You will be asked to learn the technical use of five familiar terms and to check your progress by taking a few short quizzes along the way. The chapter is really about looking at everyday life from the perspective of behavior analysis.

Changing behavior, especially when it stubbornly resists change, may require careful planning. The purpose of Chapter Four is to raise questions that need attention before proceeding with a plan of action.

Chapter Five, the heart of the book, is about forming a plan of action. The plan can provide helpful guidance when one wants to change behavior in a purposeful way. People change each others' behavior all the time in unplanned, often unconscious ways — a baby coos and inspires parental baby-talk, a teacher handles misconduct with little or no forethought. Thus planned approaches to behavior change, like the one described in this book, are unnecessary most of the time. But there are plenty of occasions when a good plan of action is essential.

The general plan grew out of the relevant literature and my experience as a behavior consultant. I started out with three key steps: define, measure, and apply strategies. Over the years I found it necessary to add steps. Role playing (rehearsing) basic features of the plan turned out to be a very important addition. I discovered that people often learn more quickly when they are shown, as well as told, what to do — for example, role playing a time-out procedure in private before implementing it in public, or showing parents how to record mock data before activating a home-school contract. Rehearsal enables participants to experience conditions much like those they will experience when a plan is put into effect. Immediate feedback for participants' efforts can then be provided. Such feedback is lacking when people are merely told what to do.

Chapter Five takes readers through each step of the plan and includes many practical examples. The sections on defining, motivation, and strategies are especially critical. These are the steps — specifying problems, locating incentives, and using good plans of action — that most determine whether behavior change will occur. The chapter includes a number of effective strategies — such as the use of home-school contracts and response cards when lecturing — that may be unfamiliar to readers.

Chapter Six is the wrap-up and shows how the general plan works in practice. This is done by applying behavior principles to three cases involving: a child who acts aggressively (a behavioral excess), an adolescent said to be unmotivated (a behavioral deficit), and an unruly class (a group management problem).

# Chapter Two

# The ABC Model of Behavior

As I indicated in Chapter One, whenever we want to change behavior in some purposeful way, it is helpful to focus on the act itself and on the events that come before and after it. The tool that helps us focus on these aspects of behavior is doing an ABC analysis. Two examples may help to show how such an analysis works. The first example concentrates on academic performance; the second on homework assignments.

> A science teacher, pointing out that consumption of finite natural resources at a steadily increasing rate could mean sudden disaster for the planet, asked her students to consider the lily-pond riddle: On the first day there was one pad in the pond; the number doubled on subsequent days until the pond completely filled on the 30th day. Students were then asked, "When is the pond exactly half full?" After two students ventured incorrect answers, the teacher provided a hint: "Remember, we're concerned with the possibility of sudden disaster." A student immediately said, "On day 29." "Right," said the teacher.

In this example, the teacher's presentation of the problem, her question, and her hint were A events. The students' attempts to solve the problem were B events, while corrective feedback from the teacher was a C event.

> Scott often promised to do his homework "later," but he seldom got around to it. So his parents set up the fol-

11

lowing rule: "First you complete your assignments, then you can hang out with your friends." After a few shaky weeks, Scott began completing assignments soon after his return from school.

Scott's parents applied a well-established principle (the Premack principle, named after David Premack, who conducted a series of experimental studies). The principle says that a preferred activity can strengthen a less-favored activity if the preferred activity (joining friends in this case) follows the less-favored one (doing homework). In this case the rule was an important A event, completing assignments were B events, and getting to join friends were C events. The principle has considerable potential for preventing problems associated with procrastination.

## More About Antecedents

Why does a person turn on a television program at the same time each week? Why does an adolescent swear around his friends but not his parents? The answers lie in past learning experiences. We learn to respond to antecedent circumstances in certain ways because we have been rewarded for doing so. We learn to distinguish (discriminate) one antecedent circumstance from another when a behavior is rewarded in one situation but not another. Thus only certain antecedents come to signal the behavior.

It is not necessary for other people to be involved for an individual to learn to discriminate. For example, if one of his toy trucks pricks his finger on several occasions, a child learns to handle it with care. He learns to distinguish the hurtful truck from the others.

Most of the time, it takes several antecedent events to cue our actions. For example, a person enters an elevator after the up light comes on, the doors open, a tone sounds, and others are seen moving in the direction of the elevator.

No doubt you can think of many situations in which prior events regulated your behavior. By way of illustration, let me confess a personal example. I once found that the regular barber in the shop I patronized did a good job on my hair but not on my beard. The Wednesday barber (the regular barber was off on Wednesdays) did a much better job on my beard, or so I thought. Thus I learned to discriminate: When it was time for a haircut, I went to the regular barber; beard cuts were scheduled for Wednesdays.

The process described above is similar to what happens when a child behaves badly in the presence of one parent but not the other, or when a person says one thing in one situation but does the opposite in another. In the first case, the child has learned to discriminate between parents. Probably one parent has rewarded bad conduct while the other has not.

In the second case, a person says one thing in one setting but does the opposite in another. Often, people characterize such behavior as "hypocrisy." But in reality, the person has learned to discriminate between situations: In the first setting, the person has been rewarded for talking in a certain way; in the other, acting in a contrary way has brought rewards. Note that this explanation for "hypocrisy" examines the environmental circumstances; it does not postulate some trait or characteristic called hypocrisy that somehow resides within the person. In order to understand behavior, it is more helpful to examine the behavior, its antecedents, and its consequences than to simply use a label.

To return to my initial questions, usually a person tunes in a television show each week because he or she finds it rewarding. Hence, the time of the show exercises considerable control over the behavior patterns associated with its viewing. Likewise, we likely will find that crude language is rewarded by the adolescent's friends but not by his parents.

All day, every day, antecedents set the occasion for our actions: A mother sees cloud formations and suggests umbrellas for her children; a physician checks a patient's eyes and hands and considers certain diagnoses; a teen hears an idol's theme song and rushes to the TV set; a man searches frantically for a properly marked restroom; a woman jolts from bed at the sound of an alarm clock.

## More About Behavior

An ABC analysis requires a clear understanding of what behavior is and what it is not. *Behavior* means doing things. It means anything a person does in response to external or internal events. Behavior is sometimes overt (publicly observable) and sometimes covert (private, unobservable to the public). Seeing Rick and saying, "Hi, Rick," is an observable, overt response; sensing a toothache and thinking, "Oh no, not again," is responding to an internal, private event.

There are two kinds of overt behaviors: Verbal and motor, that is, what a person says and does.

Thinking and feeling are mainly covert behaviors. Thinking about a dinner partner is covert behavior, as is feeling joy when listening to Bach. However, covert and overt behaviors are intricately linked; a change in overt behavior likely involves a change in covert behavior. When a parent praises a child for being helpful, it may encourage more helpfulness later. That praise also may elicit pleasant feelings in the child, even though there may be no outward sign of those feelings. Although we often concentrate on overt behavior when we want to change behavior, it is important to keep in mind that covert behaviors (thinking and feeling) also may be changing as overt behaviors change. Sometimes behavior is relatively simple, but often it is a complex sequence of overt and covert acts.

If we are to respond to behavior in a consistent way, we must define it specifically. While we often talk about behavior in general terms — such as describing a friend as "intelligent," "nice," or "creative" — none of those words specifies behavior. When we describe the friend as "intelligent," we mean that we have observed her act in ways we now summarize with that word: She learns quickly, has a large vocabulary, scores well on tests, knows a lot, solves complex problems, is an accomplished artist, and so on.

## More About Consequences

In most cases, what comes after a response is as important as what comes before it. For example, a person may have been rewarded for investing in the stock market for a decade; but after suddenly losing a large sum of money, he alters his later investment practices. In the same way, a large number of prior experiences may have influenced a teacher to avoid using the Internet; but after finding an especially helpful site, she is eager to contact it again. Similarly, getting a ticket for speeding slows the driving speed of most people, while eating an unusually delicious meal in a restaurant makes a return visit likely.

Often we are unaware of how much we are affected by the events that follow or accompany our actions. We normally engage in thousands of intellectual, social, motor, and motivational acts each day, many of which are followed by consequences that maintain our actions or make them more or less likely to recur. Some of these events are *presented* (or "turned on") after an act, while others are *removed* (or "turned off"). The next chapter examines how presenting and removing events are affected by reinforcement and punishment.

# *Chapter Three*

# A Matter of Consequences

If there is a first principle of conduct, it is this: Consequences affect future performance. This principle, formulated early in the 20th century, states that the probability of a behavior is a function of the consequences that have resulted from the behavior in the past. It is, in my view, one of the most important principles in all of social science.

We act — do things — and then something happens. The consequences of what we do largely determine what we are likely to do under similar circumstances in the future. Would a piece of chalk be used (behavior) if it left no mark on the chalkboard (consequence)? Would a child continue his tantrums (response) if no one paid attention (effect)? We turn a key and an engine starts. We add a column of numbers and find a billing error. Scratching an itch brings welcome relief.

It is very easy to overlook consequences and their influence. For example, many people think that it is the arrival of an elevator that rewards a person for pressing the call button. They do not see that the panel light that the button activates is the immediate reward for pressing the button. The importance of this immediate consequence is illustrated when the light fails to come on and someone continues to press the button. The elevator's arrival is the reward for "waiting for the elevator," but the light is an important part of the chain.

Here is another example: Many behaviors correlated with age are attributed to factors originating inside the person, rather than to consequences. Young children characteristically sit before they crawl, crawl before taking first steps, and fall and bump themselves many times before learning to walk. Our physical body, of course, always has an influence on our behavior; but attributing this sequence *solely* to "maturation" or inherent ability overlooks thousands of responses and subsequent consequences that shape walking. To ignore those responses and consequences seriously impedes the analysis of behavior.

## Reinforcers

Reinforcers are consequences of fundamental importance. There are two types of reinforcers: positive and negative. Both increase the frequency or likelihood of behavior, but they do so in different ways. Positive reinforcement involves *presenting* something after a response occurs, while negative reinforcement involves *removing* or *preventing* something.

Here are two sample incidents. Do they illustrate positive or negative reinforcement?

- A comedian retains in his repertoire only those jokes that get favorable audience reactions.
- A man adds a touch of lemon extract to his German cheesecake and finds that he prefers the taste. He adds extract to all subsequent cheesecakes.

Did you decide that both episodes illustrate positive reinforcement? The comedian discovers that telling certain jokes leads to laughter, making it likely that he will tell them again in the future. As we shall see, other consequences also affect the comedian's behavior. Similarly, adding lemon extract to the cheesecake is strengthened by a subsequent event, improved taste. In both cases, something was presented after behavior (laughter, improved taste) and behavior was strengthened.

What do you make of these examples?

- Many people buckle their seat belt in order to turn off an annoying dashboard light.
- José got a smile and pat on the shoulder from his teacher after completing all the assigned math problems.

Because buckling up is maintained by removing or turning off an unwanted event (the light), the first example illustrates negative reinforcement. The second case is a bit trickier. No change in behavior is stated or implied, and so this is an indefinite situation. As far as we know, José did not change his behavior as a result of the teacher's smile and pat. This raises an important point: a reinforcer or punisher is defined by its effect on subsequent behavior, not by how it looks.

Before you respond to more cases, let me point out once again that the principles described here are applicable to desirable as well as undesirable behaviors. Here are a couple more examples:

- Sophia makes her bed each morning and thus avoids her mother's complaints.
- A teacher encourages creativity by acknowledging students' imaginative essays but not their commonplace essays. As a result, her students are writing more creatively.

Sophia avoids her mother's complaints by making her bed, thus the act of bed-making is negatively reinforced. Something is removed — the likelihood of complaints — and bed-making is maintained. Sophia herself is not negatively reinforced, her bed-making is. This restriction reminds us to focus on what a person is *doing*, on the person's actions and what follows them, not on the person. In the second case, the teacher positively reinforces innovation by recognizing only essays that she considers imaginative.

Here are some more samples to consider:

- A politician discovers that choosing her words carefully keeps her from angering constituents.
- Wilma's father (unlike her mother) very gently removes a splinter from her finger. Subsequent splinters send her running to him for help.

The politician prevents (removes the likelihood of) anger by speaking cautiously, and her audiences provide negative reinforcement for her careful talk. Wilma runs to her father because

19

doing so is negatively reinforced by the removal of something unpleasant.

The next two examples illustrate the reciprocal nature of social relationships:

- Gabe's tantrums are frequent because his parents give in to his demands.
- Gabe's parents have learned to quell his outbursts by complying with his wishes.

These examples look the same, but they are subtly different. These are examples of both positive and negative reinforcement. In the first example, because Gabe's tantrums are followed by getting what he wants, Gabe's parents are increasing the likelihood of tantrums in the future. This is positive reinforcement. In the second example, Gabe negatively reinforces his parents' actions: He simply "turns off" — stops complaining — when they give in to his demands.

As we interact with others, we often reinforce, ignore, or punish each other's behavior. Thus the last two situations reflect the reciprocal nature of social relationships: Gabe's parents reward his tantrums positively; he in turn rewards their actions negatively. This is much like what happens when a baby cries until someone picks her up: The person responding to the baby's cry positively rewards crying; the baby, by becoming calm, negatively rewards the behavior of the person coming to help.

## Escape and Avoidance

Negative reinforcement helps us understand how we learn to escape or avoid many unpleasant things in life. Suppose a student is attacked by other students as he takes his usual route home from school. He escapes by running away. On subsequent days he avoids his attackers by going home by an alternative route. Running away, because it terminates an *existing* unpleasant consequence, is escape behavior. However, taking an alternative route, because it terminates the *possibility* of an unpleasant experience, is avoidance. Escape and avoidance behaviors both involve negative reinforcement.

The concept of negative reinforcement helps us understand why people do things for which they get no apparent reward. You may know a child who generally keeps to herself, rather than joining her peers. Being alone is not considered to be very rewarding, and so the child might be said to be socially withdrawn. But if we want to know why the child avoids others, the answer may well lie in past consequences. She may have learned to deal with painful situations by avoiding them. One characteristic of avoidance behaviors is that they may occur with little or no awareness that they are based on something unpleasant. Neither the child nor the adults around her in this case may be aware that negative reinforcement is at work. Simply labeling the child shy or withdrawn will not be enough to help her.

Escape and avoidance also occur in our private thoughts. For example, we sometimes deny (escape) or avoid thoughts that make us feel anxious or guilty by turning to more pleasant things. We may even be completely unaware of this defense, which some might label "repression."

## Hidden Consequences

I have had many discussions with people who think that too much has been made of reinforcement, that it is not very important. One point they make is that students engage in a number of behaviors that are not rewarded. However, it is critical to keep three things in mind when analyzing behavior for which there is no readily apparent reward:

1. The person may be engaging in escape or avoidance. Just because nothing is presented after behavior, one should not hastily conclude that reinforcement is absent.
2. A narrow view of consequences may keep us from seeing the events in a person's life that function as rewards.
3. The behavior we see may be rewarded only occasionally, and we are not privy to those occasions.

Points 2 and 3 lead us to the topics of the *classification* and *timing* of reinforcement.

## Classifying Reinforcers

Although there is some overlap among these classifications, reinforcers may be classified into four broad categories: activity reinforcers, social reinforcers, nonconsumable tangible reinforcers, and primary (or survival) reinforcers. Punishments can be classified in the same way.

I have listed a few common reinforcers under each classification. Try adding to the lists some of the things you find rewarding. What activities do you especially enjoy? What tangibles do you prize?

| *Activity* | *Social* | *Tangible* | *Primary* |
|---|---|---|---|
| Playing | Attention | Money | Oxygen |
| Reading | Smiles | Clothing | Food |
| Watching TV | Praise | Cars | Sleep |
| Thinking | Hugs | Jewelry | Warmth |
| Jogging | Proximity | Pictures | Liquids |
| Working puzzles | Touching | Videos | Sex |

These categories have considerable practical value. They call attention to the enormous range and variety of things that serve as consequences for our actions, though the list in each category provides only a slight hint of that range and variety. For example, sensory stimulation, a very powerful primary reinforcer, does not appear on the list.

Given human nature, things that are rewarding will vary considerably from one person to another. Thus, if we are not to be misled by this variability, a broad view of possible reinforcers is needed. Some people respond positively to a kind word (social), some will complete a task for a chance to watch TV (activity), others love jewelry (tangible), while still others relish gourmet food (primary). Often more than one kind of reward follows what we do. If a son nags until his demand for the family car is met, nagging may be strengthened by the attention it brings (social), by the use of the car (tangible), and by driving itself (activity). Moreover, rewards can be just about anything — the laughter of fellow students, the sound of a dropped book, seeing an adult get angry, and being sent to the principal's office can all function as rewards for some students. I will return to these categories when I take up the topic of motivation.

## Timing of Reinforcement

Our actions are not always followed by reinforcers (or punishments). Even a highly successful bill collector is not always rewarded for his efforts; some folks just don't pay. And some drivers run red lights many times before getting caught. The occasion when reinforcement occurs can be termed "reinforcement timing." Behaviors that are attributed to, say, drives or compulsions might be better attributed to the effects of timing. If a person works long and hard on a project, for instance, she may be doing so not so much because of some inner drive or compulsion but because reinforcement becomes available to her in ways that encourage a great deal of resolve.

There are several ways in which reinforcement is timed, and they may be combined in complex ways. Such arrangements have powerful and wide-ranging effects on behavior, though their influence goes unnoticed most of the time. I describe below some everyday examples of the basic timetables of reinforcement. Each type has fairly predictable effects on behavior as long as the schedule is kept more or less constant.

*Continuous reinforcement* is when a particular behavior sequence is rewarded each time it occurs. Eating is usually reinforced continuously — before we feel full, each bite of food is rewarding. Apparatus kept in good working order also reward us continuously. Every time we turn on our television set, we are rewarded by the picture and sound.

When a person has gotten used to continuous reinforcement, any drastic change (such as complete cessation of reinforcement) may generate anger or aggression. A so-called spoiled child — say, one who has gotten a great deal of attention in the past — may throw a fit when his mother's attention is diverted, as it might be while they are both out shopping. And some people find themselves pounding a vending machine when it fails to deliver an item, even though it has given them perfect service in the past.

*Intermittent reinforcement* is common in social situations and occurs in four ways: fixed and variable ratio, fixed and variable interval. With ratio timing, reinforcement depends on the number of times a particular response occurs. If a reinforcer is delivered after a constant number of responses, the schedule is called fixed-ratio (FR); if the number varies, it is a variable-ratio (VR) timetable.

Paying people on a piece-rate basis or providing free time after students solve a fixed number of problems are examples of FR timing. VR timing is fairly prevalent in everyday life. The bill collector referred to earlier is subject to a VR schedule of reinforcement, as are athletes. For example, batting averages in baseball and percentage of baskets made at the free-throw line in basketball are numerical indicators of VR schedules.

It is common to see teachers and parents shift from continuous to VR schedules as they teach children new skills. A father may praise his young daughter for nearly every response she makes learning to tie her shoes for the first time; but at later stages of learning, his praise reflects a VR pattern.

Ratio schedules depend on one's own actions. Consider the bill collector once again. His skill and level of activity determine when and how often he receives payment; the more skillful the contacts he makes, the greater the likelihood of collecting an overdue account. With interval schedules, on the other hand, the passage of time largely determines whether a particular response is rewarded; what the person does during this time is not very important.

In fixed interval (FI) timing, the first correct response after a fixed period of time is reinforced. A child who is praised every 15 minutes for productive practice is on an FI schedule.

Waiting for an elevator involves variable interval (VI) timing. On one occasion, standing by the elevator is rewarded by the arrival of the elevator after, say, 10 seconds; on another occasion, after 126 seconds; and on still another, after 48 seconds, and so on. What the person does while waiting has no influence on the arrival of the elevator.

Variable schedules can have a strong influence on behavior. The obsession of gamblers (VR) and the football aficionado who sits glued to his television set (VI) are mysteries only to those who are unaware of the power of variable schedules to generate frequent and stable performance.

The timing of reinforcement in daily life often occurs in complex combinations. For example, a salesman on salary and commission is subject to mixed FI and FR schedules. Mixed patterns of reward in daily life are likely to be quite difficult to identify and interpret.

## Discontinuation of Reinforcement

Thus far this chapter has focused on reinforcement and various types of reinforcers. But what happens when reinforcement is no longer available?

When a reward that once maintained a particular behavior is discontinued or withheld, the behavior is likely to weaken or decline in frequency. This process is called *extinction*. An earlier example of positive reinforcement was illustrated by the comedian who kept certain jokes in his routine because audiences liked them. Actually, extinction also was involved. While some jokes brought warm applause and laughter and were therefore reinforced, others were met with agonizing silence. Jokes consistently greeted by silence were dropped (extinguished) from the comedian's repertoire. In another previous example, Gabe's parents rewarded tantrums by giving Gabe what he wanted. If, instead, they could have managed to ignore *every* tantrum, the tantrums would have disappeared (been extinguished). In extinction, one must withhold reinforcement every time a behavior occurs, otherwise an intermittent schedule will be in effect. This point is important because intermittent schedules, unlike continuous schedules, tend to make a person pursue things more persistently.

One additional feature of extinction merits mention. Avoidance behaviors, because they are maintained by negative reinforcement, are stubbornly resistant to the extinction process. Perhaps this is so because avoidance keeps one from learning — through extinction — that once painful stimuli are no longer a threat. For example, a person's fears of public speaking cannot be extinguished if he or she never gets up in front of a group to speak.

## Punishment

Extinction is not the only way learned behaviors are weakened or eliminated. Punishment is another way. Psychologists are in general agreement that punishment can be effective but should be used sparingly and with caution.

There are two types of punishment. Positive punishment is when an event is presented, or "turned on," and a response is thereby weakened (decreases in frequency or likelihood). Negative punishment is when an event is removed, or "turned off," after a response, weakening the response. In other words, positive punishment presents something unpleasant, while negative punishment takes away something pleasant. Both procedures weaken the response.

You may have noticed a certain parallelism between positive/negative reinforcement and positive/negative punishment. In both cases, positive means *presenting* something and negative means *removing* something. In the case of reinforcement, what is presented is something desirable, while what is removed is something undesirable. A punishment procedure is the reverse: What is presented is undesirable; what is removed is desirable.

Following is a self-test. Do the situations illustrate positive or negative punishment?

- A comedian drops from his routine those jokes that audiences boo.

- Shelly's mother fined Shelly one dollar each time she used crude language in front of her little brother. Shelly stopped just short of losing a week's allowance.

In the first situation, because audiences boo (present unpleasantries) after hearing a joke, the joke is dropped. This fits the definition of positive punishment. We have met the comedian in previous examples. Notice how audiences have shaped his performance by using positive reinforcement (for funny material) and positive punishment and extinction (for unfunny stuff).

In Shelly's case, something desirable (one dollar) was removed each time she used crude language in front of her brother. Since the crude language stopped, negative punishment was at work.

Two more examples may be helpful.

- As Alessandra reached for the cookie jar, her mother said, "Get your hand away from there!" Reaching stopped.
- On two occasions Jeff got his hand slapped as he reached for a toy on display. He no longer reaches for things on display unless he first gets permission.

Alessandra and Jeff have experienced positive punishment because, in both cases, something was presented and the behavior weakened. Punishment was verbal in the first episode and physical in the second. Jeff's situation demonstrates an important outcome of punishment. If we say that asking permission is an avoidance response, then we can see how punishment and negative reinforcement go hand in hand: Asking permission was negatively reinforced because it prevented further contact with a punishing event.

Here's one more example:

- Whenever little Benjamin jumped up and down on the living room couch, the television was turned off for two minutes. He got the message rather quickly.

Negative punishment accounts for the cessation of Benjamin's jumping. The television was turned off. Then the jumping stopped.

This case demonstrates an important point. The removal of a reward was punishment. When desirable behavior (not jumping) occurred, the reward (television) was made available. The availability of a reward in negative punishment is one reason why this type of punishment may be preferred over positive punishment in many situations.

## Problems with Punishment

Discontinuing punishment may lead to the resumption of the previously punished behavior. Recall that Shelly was fined one dollar each time she used crude language in front of her younger brother. She eventually stopped. But she may refrain from crude speech only if the possibility of a fine continues to exist. Thus punishment may suppress but not eliminate behavior.

There is ample evidence to support the position that punishment may not be the best way to stop or prevent undesirable behavior. Delinquency, one of the most disturbing and extensive problems in childhood and adolescence, provides a good example. Punitive programs have long been used as a way of coping with delinquent behavior, but these programs have had a depressing history. While punishment may suppress unlawful activity, its effect is not permanent in far too many cases. Many delinquents simply learn to avoid getting caught and punished. When away from the watchful eyes of parents and other authority figures, their unlawful behaviors reappear, maintained by supportive peers and by various rewards associated with the criminal activity itself.

Recent work with delinquents appears to be on the right track when it encourages removing youth from situations that may allow or encourage bad behavior. Programs that remove youth from situations that may encourage delinquency and place them in settings where they can learn desirable behaviors — such as academic, athletic, occupational, and communicative skills — are more likely to show positive results than do programs preoccupied with punishment.

There are a number of additional problems associated with the use of punishment. For example, when we use punishment — especially positive punishment — we risk eliciting negative emotional reactions that linger beyond the punishing incident itself, possibly for days, weeks, months, even years. Such reactions can be lethal to human relationships. A father who harshly punishes his son, for example, might stop his son's misconduct, but he also might alienate him emotionally. Punishment lets the misbehaving individual know that something is wrong but often fails to teach acceptable behaviors. I say more about punishment in Chapter Five.

## Self-Test

Following is a way to determine understanding of the concepts in this chapter. Do the situations that follow illustrate positive reinforcement, negative reinforcement, extinction, positive punishment, negative punishment, or none of these? An answer key follows the self-test.

1. Carol's parents ignored her attempts to talk about school. She no longer brings the subject up.
2. Frank used to greet his colleague with friendly "hellos" and similar expressions. His greetings were met with sarcastic comments. After several such incidents, Frank stopped speaking to his colleague.
3. Julie's new haircut brought rave reviews. She has decided to adopt her new coiffure permanently.
4. John touched Ellen. She hauled off and slapped him. As a result, he touches her more often.
5. Juan liked doing the weekly grocery shopping when he was first married. On most occasions, though, he was criticized on his return home for forgetting items, paying too much, and so on. He now scrupulously avoids shopping.
6. Don was sued for malpractice and lost; he now refrains from actions that led to the litigation.
7. Vicky pays her gas bills on time in order to avoid a late fee.

8. A teacher got her students to pay no attention to Al whenever he clowned around. It worked. Al has found other ways to get attention.
9. Most people stop at traffic lights to avoid accidents, attention from the police, and so on.
10. Emily got a hug and pat on the back for (finally) completing her assignment.
11. Because a government bureaucrat had a surplus in her budget the previous year, the subsequent allocation for her department was reduced by a corresponding amount. She has since abandoned her frugal ways.
12. By building novelty and conflict into their stories, newscasters have found they can attract and hold audiences.

## Answer Key

1. Carol's attempts to talk about school were ignored — attention was withheld. This illustrates extinction. Carol's parents (probably unthinkingly) extinguished Carol's positive behavior.
2. Frank stopped talking to his colleague because speaking was followed by unfriendly comments. Frank's greetings were positively punished.
3. Positive reinforcement appears to explain Julie's decision to make a permanent change in hair style.
4. This was a trick question. Remember, reinforcers and punishers are identified *by their effect on behavior*, not by their appearance. Although the slap should have been a positive punishment, it turned out to be a positive reinforcer.
5. Positive punishment (nagging criticism) appears to have been the key factor in eliminating Juan's trips to the grocery store.
6. After losing money in court, Don no longer engages in the practice for which he was negatively punished.
7. Vicky pays on time to prevent a penalty (having money "removed"). Paying on time is thus negatively reinforced.

8. The teacher and her students have successfully applied an extinction procedure.
9. Stopping at traffic signals is essentially avoidance behavior and thus maintained by negative reinforcement.
10. Without more information, we don't know how the hug and pat affected Emily. This question, with a different name (José), was asked at the beginning of the chapter. Subsequent behavior is necessary before we can determine what happened, if anything, as a result of the hug.
11. The bureaucrat has been negatively punished for being fiscally responsible.
12. The newscasters are being rewarded by two very powerful, positive reinforcers: audience attention and money (large audiences, large profits).

# *Chapter Four*

## Preliminary Concerns

My purpose in this very brief chapter is to raise some important questions that need to be considered before proceeding with a general plan of action for changing behavior.

### Ethical Considerations

Whether you are a teacher, a parent, a nurse, or a therapist, the following kinds of questions need to be raised before executing a plan to change someone's behavior.

Will a change in behavior serve the best interest of the person — his or her intellectual, emotional, and social well-being?

Am I competent to deal with the problem? Can I be objective?

Does the person have a realistic chance of reaching the program goals. That is, are there medical or other complications that might make success unlikely? (Smoking cessation springs to mind. A long-standing smoking habit is pretty resistant to change. As I indicated in Chapter One, some behavior change should be left to specialists.)

Will I be using the most humane procedures possible? Will the person be informed about the plan and consent to it?

Am I violating any of the person's civil rights? It is not acceptable, for example, to deprive a person of food or other basic necessities as a means to motivate behavior change. It also is inadvisable in nonclinical settings to use food or other primary reinforcers to make people conform. Nor is it acceptable to tamper, say, with a student's right of free speech.

These are important, albeit difficult, questions. But they must be considered before embarking on a plan to change behavior.

## Background Information

A second concern is obtaining background information before beginning a behavior change plan. It is important to get information *directly* related to the behavior with which you plan to work. Here are five questions that need at least preliminary answers:

1. How long has the behavior been going on (or how long has there been a deficiency)?
2. How has it been dealt with in the past?
3. Under what conditions does it occur?
4. How often does it occur?
5. What usually happens immediately after it occurs?

The first question tells us something about how hard it may be to change behavior. If the problem behavior has a long history, your task may be relatively difficult. With the second question, you may find that a number of things have been tried in the past with little or no success. Perhaps attempts to change behavior have been ill-conceived, inconsistent, mismanaged, or simply too short-lived to be effective. Parents sometimes abandon good strategies simply because they cannot withstand a child's complaints. On the other hand, sometimes the sources of difficulty have been identifying effective incentives or establishing links between incentives and behavior.

The last three questions in particular should sound familiar. They relate to the components of the ABC model that I discussed in Chapter Two and are important for reasons I gave previously: Whenever we want to teach anybody anything they are capable of learning, we must pay close attention to antecedent conditions, how the person responds in the presence of these conditions, and what happens afterward.

Finally, as you gather background information directly related to your task, you may find it helpful to consult relevant literature to see how others have dealt with the problem in which you are interested. The behavior change literature encompasses a wide variety of people and activities, such as parent-child relationships, instruction and classroom conduct, health and medical care, athletic performance, behavior therapy for adults and children, suggestions for self-improvement, and much more. A list of suggested reading is included at the end of this chapter.

Once you have plausible answers to these questions, you can decide how, or whether, to proceed. If you decide to continue, you need at some point to identify the people who will be involved in your plan. Who will help you with the plan? Who might hinder it? Teachers, administrators, parents, siblings, relatives, and friends are all people who can make or break a behavior change program.

In the next chapter I will discuss making a behavior change plan, including how to develop a behavior contract. The important thing to remember at this juncture is to enlist the help of key individuals in designing the behavior change plan. People are more likely to support programs they have helped to design. Designing and implementing behavior contracts, for instance, typically involve two or more people — including the subject of the contract. Thoughtful contracts have a good chance of working when the people involved have a hand in their construction.

## Suggested Reading

Baldwin, John D., and Baldwin, Janice I. *Behavior Principles in Everyday Life*. 3rd ed. Englewood Cliffs, N.J.: Prentice-Hall, 1998.

Written by two sociologists, this book provides hundreds of plausible and interesting examples of how behavioral concepts and principles are relevant to our daily lives.

Martin, Garry, and Pear, Joseph. *Behavior Modification: What It Is and How to Do It*. 6th ed. Englewood Cliffs, N.J.: Prentice-Hall, 1999.

I highly recommend this book. Martin and Pear provide valuable details and guidelines for the implementation of strategies. They also delve into such topics as thinking, feeling, private behavior, and clinical behavior therapy.

Sloane, Howard N. *The Good Kid Book: How to Solve the 16 Most Common Problems.* Champaign, Ill.: Research Press, 1988.

This is a very helpful book, especially for parents. It offers step-by-step ways to deal with whining, shyness, arguing, disobedience, homework problems, and much more. Readers need not read the entire book to find out what to do about a problem.

*Journals:*

Several journals regularly publish articles concerned with behavior change. The four listed below are especially recommended for teachers and parents:

*Behavior Modification*
Sage Publications, Inc.
2455 Teller Rd.
Thousand Oaks, CA 91320
(805) 499-0721
Fax: (805) 499-0871
Email: order@sagepub.com
website: www.sagepub.com

*Behavior Therapy*
Association for Advancement of Behavior Therapy
305 Seventh Ave,
New York, NY 10001
(212) 647-1890
Fax: (212) 647-1865
website: www.aabt.org/aabt

*Education and Treatment of Children*
PRO-ED
8700 Shoal Creek Blvd.
Austin, TX 78757
1-800-897-3202
Fax: 1-800-397-7633
Email: proed1@aol.com
website: www.proedinc.com

*Journal of Applied Behavior Analysis*
Society for the Experimental Analysis of Behavior, Inc.
Department of Psychology
Indiana University
Bloomington, IN 47405
*subscriptions:*
Department of Human Development
University of Kansas
Lawrence, KS 66045
(785) 843-0008
Fax: (785) 843-5909
Email: jabamlw@idir.net
website: www.envmed.rochester.edu/wwwrap/behavior/jaba/
        jabahome.htm

*General Information Sources:*
Research Press
Department 99
P.O. Box 9177
Champaign, IL 61826
1-800-519-2707
Fax: (217) 352-1221
Email: rp@researchpress.com
website: www.researchpress.com


This publisher is an important source for practical training and
teaching materials. It offers an extensive line of books and media
programs on classroom management, special education, counsel-

ing and therapy, and family life and parenting. Several books and videos focus on the strategies for increasing and decreasing behaviors touched on in this book. A good basic video is *Behavioral Principles for Parents*, which presents for discussion 31 realistic vignettes of parent-child interactions. The video is useful in teaching the correct and incorrect use of reinforcement and punishment.

PRO-ED
8700 Shoal Creek Blvd.
Austin, TX 78757
1-800-897-3202
Fax: 1-800-397-7633
Email: proed1@aol.com
website: www.proedinc.com

This publisher's "How to Manage Behavior" series features 15 titles that provide nontechnical, step-by-step procedures for changing the behavior of children and adults in a variety of home, school, and job settings. Each short manual teaches a particular strategy, such as time-out, response cost, overcorrection, planning for generalization (transfer), and performance contracting. Parents, teachers, and therapists will find this series quite useful.

# *Chapter Five*

# A General Plan for Behavior Change

In this chapter I describe a nine-step plan for changing behavior. Recall that the plan is the second phase of a two-stage process: First an ABC analysis is done, then the following plan is set in motion.

Describing steps in a plan is very much easier, of course, than implementing them; but if you are alert and conservative in your approach, if you learn to "walk before you run," you can be successful in changing behavior. People who are competent in changing behavior are flexible and creative in applying basic principles; they know there are no handy, sure-fire recipes that can be rigidly applied.

A proviso is in order. Although this plan is presented in nine steps, the number of steps — and even their order — is not sacred. Sometimes the plan can be put into effect easily by simply specifying a behavior (Step 1), applying a strategy (Step 7), and noting the result (Step 8). At other times, most or all nine steps may be necessary. Sometimes, too, the entire plan can be implemented in a few minutes, as in the case of the elementary school teacher I will describe in a moment. In other cases it may be essential for the plan to be applied over several weeks or months. In short, the plan is to be used "artistically," rather than "mechanically," for the optimum results.

## Nine Steps

Step 1: Define behavior.
Step 2: Estimate its amount.

Step 3: Set attainable goals.
Step 4: Identify potential reinforcers.
Step 5: Select teaching procedures.
Step 6: Rehearse key elements.
Step 7: Implement the plan.
Step 8: Monitor results.
Step 9: Maintain and generalize gains.

This plan is appropriate whenever we are dealing with too much behavior (an excess), too little (a deficit), or inappropriate behavior. Physical aggression, monopolizing conversations, overeating, and watching television many hours each day are candidates for behavioral excess; low motivation, painful shyness, and not completing tasks exemplify deficits. Breaches in etiquette, such as telling jokes in church or complaining to the party host ("awful food") are considered improper on most occasions and thus are inappropriate. Deciding what is too much, too little, or inappropriate requires a judgment call. Being assertive, for example, may or may not be a problem. It depends on circumstances: If assertiveness is too frequent, that is one type of problem; if it is not frequent enough, that may be another problem.

The plan is applicable not only for changing someone else's behavior but also for changing one's own. All of us are subject to the kinds of excesses and deficits I just mentioned, with large variations in kind and degree. When we want to change some aspect of our behavior — stop drinking too much, stop being late to work, start being nicer to one's spouse, start regular exercise — we may resort to "willpower." But willpower alone, as most of us have learned, does not always work. What we actually may need is to change our physical and social environment so that it affects us differently, thus bringing about a change in what we do. This is an apt description of self-control from a behavior analytic perspective: To change behavior, change the environment so that it becomes enabling in a positive way, rather than in a negative way.

As we take a closer look at the plan, keep in mind that it also may be useful in a personal, self-improvement program. Each of us can, for example, specify a behavior we want to change (to jog regularly), estimate its current amount (less than a mile per week), set a distant goal (15 miles per week), and so on.

## Putting the Plan to Work

Consider the case of a kindergarten teacher. Her pupils were having trouble moving from one activity to another in an orderly manner. The problem was most obvious during transition from free play to story time, when the children ignored requests to put away toys and settle down for story time. When asked, the teacher would say that the children loved hearing the stories, but getting them settled often took 10 minutes or more.

This case demonstrates the usefulness of an ABC analysis: Before the plan was activated, teacher instructions (A events) were ineffective in getting students to put away toys and remain quiet (B events), and noncompliance was rewarded by reading stories immediately after delays occurred (C events).

Things improved when the teacher followed this plan. She told the students, "When free time ends, I will turn the room lights off for two minutes. When I turn them back on, all toys are to be put away and everyone is to be sitting quietly and waiting for story time. If everyone is not ready, we will have to have story time later in the day." This was essentially a negative punishment procedure. The teacher also role-played acceptable and unacceptable behavior and praised those youngsters who complied, where previously the stragglers got most of her attention.

Subsequently, teacher requests (A) became associated with a new event, lights off (A), while compliance (B) was rewarded with stories and praise (C). In effect, the teacher began rewarding compliance rather than noncompliance. This case also shows how a behavior change plan can easily be implemented (literally in a matter of minutes) and can fit naturally into a daily routine.

Even though the teacher did not articulate the nine steps, they were all present:

Step 1: Define behavior.
*Toys put away; sitting quietly.*

Step 2: Estimate its amount.
*Delays occurred daily.*
Step 3: Set attainable goals.
*Students ready in two minutes.*
Step 4: Identify potential reinforcers.
*Story time (activity); praise (social).*
Step 5: Select teaching procedures.
*Verbal instruction; lights off and on; praise for compliance; punishment for delay.*
Step 6: Rehearse key elements.
*Several role-plays.*
Step 7: Implement the plan.
*Done after role-plays.*
Step 8: Monitor results.
*Plan worked from start.*
Step 9: Maintain and generalize gains.
*Cueing with lights gradually eliminated in favor of teacher directives; praise continued; occasional extra stories as bonuses.*

It would be nice if all problems were solved as easily as this one was. But complex problems require more attention to each step in the plan. Following are other, more taxing examples.

## Step 1: Define Behavior

A couple of years ago, a six-year-old boy made national news when he was portrayed as a sexual harasser because he kissed a girl on the cheek. How could this have happened? It happened, in my view, because his adult accusers were confused about the behaviors and conditions that constitute sexual harassment. There is a transparent message in this case: Labels and general terms affixed to vaguely understood behaviors can do more harm than good.

Before we can work with a problem behavior in a consistent way, it must be defined. Many behaviors are relatively easy to define — cussing, self-reference (I, me, my, mine, myself), spelling errors, and chores completed or neglected. On the other hand, many behaviors — being off-task, verbal abuse, shyness, and arguing — are more difficult to define.

Good definitions, first of all, are clear and specific. This means that your description of a behavior enables others to observe the same behavior and draw the same conclusion. You should be able to count the behavior (How often does it occur within five minutes, 15 minutes, and so on?) or determine how long it lasts. Good definitions refer to behaviors that can be seen or heard or touched (for example, feeling someone's taut neck muscles). Terms that only imply behavior should be exchanged for those that refer to directly observable action. For example, does "bad attitude" refer to talking back to a teacher, failure to complete assignments, calling other children unflattering names, or perhaps all of these actions? Clarity and specificity require that we name these behaviors, not lump them together under a generic label such as "bad attitude."

Definitions also should be as complete as possible. And others should agree that a definition adequately represents a problem behavior. The adults who charged the six-year-old child with sexual harassment failed on at least two counts: They were not clear about the meaning of sexual harassment nor could they (thankfully) get others to agree with their bizarre definition.

Here are two examples: To describe a student as "very aggressive" is neither clear nor specific. People can be verbally or physically aggressive or both. And one can be verbally and physically aggressive in many different ways. Verbal aggression involves swearing in some cases, sarcasm in others. Some physically aggressive people will scratch and pull hair; others will punch, kick, and slap. To determine what "very aggressive" means, we must find out what the person *does* and *how often*. As you watch a person closely, you may find that a child is physically but not verbally aggressive — he hits with open and closed hands, shoves, and kicks. These behaviors can be counted and recorded. In fact, if you cannot count or measure these acts in some efficient way, you have not adequately defined physical aggression.

Defining physical aggression in terms of hitting, shoving, and kicking is adequate if that is all the person does. But it is incomplete if the person also throws things, pulls hair, and threatens peers verbally. As part of defining, finally, check to see whether others who have seen the person act aggressively (teachers, parents, administrators, possibly the subject himself) believe the definition makes sense.

In the second example, calling someone "plain lazy" is an inadequate definition of behavior. How can we count "lazy"? We can change "lazy" to "unmotivated" and make it sound more professional, but it still is only a vague description, not a definition of behavior. How would you *measure* "unmotivated"? We must be specific about what a person does or does not do to merit the label. Does the student lose assignment sheets, fail to read when asked to do so, stare out the window instead of working on the assignment, and so on? These are observable phenomena; they can be seen, counted, and recorded; they can be verified by others.

Notice that if good definitions require that we focus on what a person does, it follows that definitions must make use of direct, simple, action verbs — verbs that direct our attention to behaviors that can be observed and measured or counted. "Hitting," "kicking," and "shoving" are action verbs in this sense, as are "talking," "writing," "running," "singing," "sighing," and "painting." However, words such as "thinking," "appreciating," "understanding," and "learning" are abstract and complex; they do not serve well in describing specific behavior.

Defining behavior in observable and measurable terms is the foundation of the behavior analytic approach to changing behavior. In formulating a definition, it is important to observe how a person behaves in a variety of situations. While observing, don't forget the other components of the ABC model. Try to find out when and where the behavior occurs (antecedents) and pay close attention to the rewards (consequences) that keep it going. In the case of aggression, one might first observe the individual in several settings where he has acted aggressively (classroom, gym, playground). A definition could then be developed by describing the specific actions judged to be aggressive.

The following chart offers a few sample definitions of select terms to illustrate how behavior can be described clearly and specifically. Note that the verbs used direct attention to observable acts.

| Setting | Term | Sample Definition |
|---|---|---|
| Student asks for help in class | Well-mannered | Says "please," "thank you," "may I." Speaks slowly and softly. |
| Football coach asked to state most important player characteristic | Good attitude | Shows up at all practice sessions; hustles; does extra warm ups; talks positively about team and coach. |
| Student who keeps to herself in school | Shy | Speaks only when spoken to; eats alone; keeps physical distance from others (three or more feet). |
| Parent highly critical of family members | Verbal abuse | Swears at members; speaks negatively of their dress, looks, opinions, friends. |
| Student in science class | Off-task | Motor off-task (passes objects, taps pencil); verbal off-task (talks); visual off-task (looks away from task five or more seconds). |

The information in this chart may seem to be fairly obvious, but do not take behavior for granted. Sometimes I ask my students, some of whom are practicing teachers, to define "out-of-seat behavior," something they have seen many times. Although out-of-seat behavior can be observed easily, some teachers have difficulty defining it in clear and specific terms. Here is a typical example: "Out-of-seat is when the student leaves his seat to sharpen his pencil, walk around the room, or disturb others." When I ask whether, according to this definition, the student is engaged in out-of-seat behavior when the teacher gives him permission to leave or when he has moved his seat to an unassigned location or when he is kneeling in his-seat, they begin to see the need for revision.

A better definition of "out-of-seat behavior" might be: "The student is out-of-seat whenever he is not physically sitting in an assigned seat, which is in an assigned location. However, the student will not be considered out-of-seat if he has first obtained permission to leave the assigned seat." Of course, other definitions are possible, but the point about specificity of definition should be clear from this example.

## Step 2: Estimate Amount

This step requires you to estimate the current amount of behavior in some simple way. The first procedure is to determine a baseline. Establishing a baseline may take anywhere from a few seconds to four or five days, depending on the amount of behavioral fluctuation. For example, a person's weight fluctuates little from day to day, so a baseline weight would take only moments to establish. A parent might estimate that her child whines a dozen or so times per day without taking pains to count each incident, or a teacher might simply note that Jimmy wanders too much and move on from there. On the other hand, many behaviors, from physical aggression to completed homework assignments, fluctuate widely from day to day. In these cases you may need to observe behavior over several days in order to establish a baseline.

It is important to take this step seriously. Sometimes merely monitoring behavior is enough to spark a behavior change. For example, some individuals have found that simply keeping track of everything they eat helps them avoid certain foods, while others report that counting how often they gripe about something motivates a change for the better. Similarly, posting students' records of progress is likely to reward past achievement and encourage future performance. And, as many writers have found, keeping track of how many words they write each day bolsters

46

their efforts to continue. In short, many of us gain a measure of control over important aspects of our lives simply by attending to what we do — or fail to do — often by keeping short, simple, daily records.

When we want to make more accurate and complete observations of behavior, we can turn to *automatic, indirect,* and *direct* methods. The resulting information can then be shown on a simple chart or graph. Charts and graphs help us see what behavior looks like before (Step 2) and after intervention (Step 8).

*Automatic* recording includes videotaping and electronic timing devices. A videotape of a class engaged in discussion can be analyzed repeatedly to assess student interactions. A long-distance telephone bill illustrates automatic recording in work and home settings. Accuracy is the hallmark of automatic recording, though various mechanical devices may not be available or flexible enough for many situations. Someday learning may be heavily monitored with technological devices that will make sophisticated feedback available on an individual basis; if so, automatic recording will play an increasingly important part in formal education.

*Indirect* information comes from the products, records, or outcomes of people's actions — where the result of behavior is noted, not behavior itself. Teachers have always been especially interested in student products and records, often interpreting them numerically in terms of frequency (Sue turned in four homework assignments this month), rate (Jean reads 150 words per minute), or percentage (Cary got 84% of the answers correct). Parents also attend to outcomes of their children's behavior (mud tracks on the kitchen floor, an empty ice cream container in the freezer). And we know something about Plato's thinking only because of products that he left (his *Republic*, for example). Other important ways to observe indirectly include interview records, data from a behavior rating scale, and results from intelligence tests, questionnaires, and so on.

*Direct* observation is when we personally observe and record behavior *while* it is occurring. This is an important distinction, because indirect observation is at least a step removed from actually observing behavior. Thus information from indirect methods may be less reliable than information from direct methods. Several useful direct observation methods are described below:

*Narrative recording* involves taking copious notes while (or immediately after) observing behavior. Suppose a colleague, concerned about discipline, invites you to his classroom to help spot problems. If you are unsure what to look for, consider several 10- to 15-minute narrative recording sessions. Later you can subject your notes to an ABC analysis, possibly revealing one or two behaviors (and their antecedents and consequences) on which your colleague may need to concentrate.

*Frequency recording* involves simply counting how often a behavior occurs. Using the definition developed in Step 1 of the plan, you are now in a position to count how often someone hits his little sister, swears, or does a good deed. Frequency can be a good measure to use because it includes all incidents of behavior. (Strictly speaking, counting correct answers on student papers is product, not frequency, recording because students' responses occurred earlier.) It is sometimes necessary to attend to both frequency and time spent observing. Suppose, as a rough estimate of social maturity (or egocentricity), you counted the number of self-references a colleague made over a period of time in a variety of settings. On the first day you observed for 60 minutes and counted 60 instances; the corresponding numbers in the same settings for day two were 50 self-references in 25 minutes. When observing behavior for different amounts of time, as in this example, *rate of response* is called for: Simply divide frequency by observation time — for example 50 self-references in 25 minutes would equal a rate of 2 per minute ($50 \div 25 = 2$). These rates offer a more accessible picture of self-reference than do raw frequency for these two observations.

*Duration recording* involves taking note of how long a behavior lasts. You will find duration useful when measuring many behaviors, such as time spent in parallel play or on the computer, practicing, staring into space, working on a project, and so on. I once used this method in a dispute with my son. Disagreeing on the length of his showers, I decided to record their duration over several days. He started taking shorter showers after learning that they averaged 23 minutes. (How many other disputes in everyday life might be resolved if good data were available?)

*Latency recording* is noting the time between the onset of a signal or cue and the response to it. An example of latency is the response time a person takes to answer the telephone. Some people typically answer after two or three rings, while others consistently take longer. Latency can be a very useful measure of compliance or non-compliance, as in the classroom when teachers direct students and students comply. Saying that someone takes (on average) more than eight minutes to follow simple directions is saying a lot, and saying it clearly. A program can then be set up to reduce compliance time to something more reasonable.

*Interval recording* requires that each observation session be divided into equal intervals of time (usually seconds). One then notes whether a behavior occurs at any time during each interval. As an example, suppose you wanted to measure off-task behavior. You would divide, say, a 15-minute observational period into sixty 15-second intervals and simply record whether or not the person is on or off task (according to your definition) during each interval. The first two minutes (eight 15-second intervals) might be shown as follows, with X representing off-task behavior. Blanks represent on-task behavior.

| X | X | X | X | X |  |  | X |
|---|---|---|---|---|---|---|---|

This record shows that the student was off task entirely during the first minute of observation and on task only half the time during the second minute. Computed as a percentage of off-task time, the student was off task for 75% of this observation period.

*Time sampling* is easier to use than interval recording because it does not require as much continuous observation. Therefore I tend to recommend it more often than interval recording for busy teachers and parents. Time-sampling also divides observation sessions into equal intervals, but the intervals are longer — 10,

15, or 20 minutes. To use time-sampling, simply look in on behavior for a moment or two *at the end* of each interval. A principal, for example, might observe students in a particular classroom for 30 seconds every 30 minutes throughout the day to see how many students are engaged in a given activity. One way to manage this type of observation is to set an alarm watch to signal the observation period. Time sampling, like interval recording, can yield numerical results that show the percent of time (intervals) students are engaged or not engaged in some behavior. Parents checking periodically to see whether their children are studying or playing safely is a example of casual time sampling.

Some general guidelines for using these methods are important to remember. Counting behavior gives a complete picture, and you should use frequency or rate whenever you can. You can count the number of questions asked, complaints voiced, pages read, words spoken, commercials aired, students late, compliments received, adjectives used, and so on. But what about playing or studying or watching television? Can you count these? Since these and many other behaviors are continuous or ongoing, rather than discrete events, they cannot be counted. Take out-of-seat time, for example. When out-of-seat time is discrete (getting up and sitting back down are clear moments, and the out-of-seat behavior lasts about the same length of time at each occurrence), it can be counted. But when out-of-seat time is not discrete, which is more often the case, it cannot be counted. For example, noting that Billy was out of his seat only twice can obscure the fact that it was for six minutes the first time and 23 minutes the second time. With this and other nondiscrete behaviors, duration, interval, and time sampling are more accurate.

Keep in mind that time measures also can have drawbacks. For example, in time sampling, because the observation is made at the end of an interval, behavior that occurs at some other time will be missed. This drawback argues for using time sampling in cases when behavior occurs frequently. Behavior that occurs only infrequently may be missed entirely by this method.

With a little practice, direct observation becomes easy to use. Displaying the collected information will be quite helpful because you can see at a glance the behavior trends over time. A simple chart or graph is sufficient in most cases. Charts and graphs showing performance over several days or weeks can reduce a tendency that many people have to interpret natural, slight variations in behavior as more important than they are.

The "Parent Record Card" is a simple chart that a parent might use for monitoring their child's behavior with regard to time-sensitive activities, such as getting up, going to school, going to bed, and so on. This chart can be helpful in changing the child's behavior at home, but it also can be a useful device for communicating with the child's teacher when similar behavior is noticed at school.

In the sample, Tyson is a nine-year-old who tends to dawdle, according to his mother. Tyson disagrees and thinks his mother simply nags him too much. His mother makes a checklist of behaviors in question. After a week, Tyson and his mother can talk about the behaviors that have been pinpointed on the chart.

A counterpart is the "Teacher Record Card," shown in the next sample. Aretha is a high school student whose teacher believes

**Parent Record Card**

Name: Tyson

| Behavior | M | T | W | Th | F |
|---|---|---|---|---|---|
| Up on time | | ✓ | ✓ | | ✓ |
| Bed made | | ✓ | | | ✓ |
| Breakfast on time | ✓ | | | ✓ | |
| To school on time | ✓ | ✓ | | ✓ | |
| Home on time | ✓ | | ✓ | ✓ | |
| Homework completed | ✓ | ✓ | ✓ | | |
| Total checks | 4 | 4 | 3 | 3 | 2 |

that her interruptions during class discussions are disturbing the flow of instruction and holding back the other students. The teacher develops a checklist that defines "interruptive talk" and then records instances of interruption over a five-day span, choosing different discussion periods each day. In the "Rate/Minute" column of the checklist, the teacher computes the rate by dividing the number of interruptions by the number of minutes. For example, on Monday there were 15 interruptions during a 30-minute discussion for a rate of 0.5 ($15 \div 30 = 0.5$). In this case, Aretha's interruptions are most frequent on Tuesday and Friday, reaching a rate of about one every minute on the latter day.

| Teacher Record Card | | | |
|---|---|---|---|
| Name: Aretha | | | |
| Behavior: Interruptive talk: Talking while teacher or others talking | | | |
| Where/When: Science. Throughout period | | | |
| Possible Rewards: Escape from work (negative reinforcement). Socializing (positive reinforcement) | | | |
| Day | Number | Time | Rate/Minute |
| M | ЦИ ЦИ ЦИ | 10:00-10:30 | .50 |
| T | ЦИ ЦИ ЦИ II | 10:30-10:50 | .85 |
| W | ЦИ ЦИ ЦИ ЦИ | 10:15-10:45 | .66 |
| Th | ЦИ ЦИ ЦИ I | 10:00-10:30 | .53 |
| F | ЦИ ЦИ ЦИ ЦИ ЦИ ЦИ I | 10:00-10:30 | 1.0 |

## Step 3: Set Attainable Goals

Being clear about the behavior to be changed puts you in a position to consider what the behavior should look like when intervention is completed. Should one's goal be to reduce aggression to a zero level? Just how neat should an adolescent keep her room? Should Mel take the trash out every day? Should all students be required to reach mastery level (95%) in an algebra class? With behavior as serious as physical aggression, zero or near-zero levels are appropriate. But what about getting an already compulsive child to practice the violin and do her homework every day?

Setting goals must be tempered by what is appropriate and possible. Some socially withdrawn people, introverted by temperament, may not learn to interact well with others, regardless of a behavior change plan with that goal. Some young people will make great academic strides in response to special procedures, while others seemingly cannot, no matter how noble your intentions. In other words, the key word in Step 3 is *attainable*. Your task is to set goals that are neither too high nor too low, keeping in mind the best interest of the individual whose behavior is to be changed.

Two critical points should be borne in mind when setting goals. First, at a developmentally appropriate level, involve the person as an active participant in setting goals (and in designing and implementing a behavior change plan). Consider these questions: Does the person see a need for change? What does the person see as a desirable goal? Would a public or written commitment to change help the person stay on course?

Second, goal attainment often takes time. Behaviors often are not easily changed. Many learning goals can be reached only through achieving a series of subgoals. It would be unrealistic to expect someone to study three hours a day (goal) when he or she now averages only 15 minutes of daily study time. A better approach would be to increase the study time gradually, first to 20 minutes, then to half an hour, and so on. In fact, three hours a day probably is not realistic for most students below college level.

Expecting too much too quickly usually leads to disappointment, making behavior change the next time around even more difficult. One has only to consider the number of people who try and fail repeatedly to lose weight, stop smoking, save money, and so forth, to realize that gradual change, persistence, and realistic goals are extremely important to long-term success.

## Step 4: Identify Potential Reinforcers

This is one of the most important steps in a behavior change plan. In general, teachers and parents will do well to look at motivation in practical terms, focusing on corrective feedback and reinforcers. Keep in mind that potential reinforcers need to be tested. Determining whether something acts as a reinforcer is possible only by noting how it affects a person's actions. Reinforcers can energize bad behavior as readily as they energize good behavior.

Here are some things you can do to locate possible motivators. The first four are especially important.

*Direct Observation.* Watch carefully what a person does and says in as many situations or settings as possible. A child who consistently chooses hamburgers or pizza over all other foods obviously likes them. An adolescent who spends leisure time reading, talking on the telephone, listening to rock music, and playing tennis likes doing these things. On the other hand, someone might say he likes opera; but if he declines most opportunities to attend a performance or listen to recordings, we can suspect that talking about opera is more rewarding than the music itself. In looking for reinforcers, something that a person does often might serve as an important incentive later.

*Interviews.* Interviewing an individual and others who know him or her well is another way to identify potential motivators. A teacher might interview the child, the mother or father, and perhaps a former teacher. These interviews can take time, but they will be well worth the effort if they help one to discover effective incentives for change.

Interviewing the various individuals separately will preserve the independence of their responses. Ask a number of questions related to each of the reinforcer categories I discussed in Chapter Three: activity, social, tangible, and primary. For example, in the activity category you might ask: What do you like to do in your spare time? What are your favorite games? In school? At home?

What are your favorite TV programs? What do you do after school? How often do you do these things? If a child has trouble responding to direct questions, try using a list or pictures of potential reinforcers.

It should take no more than two or three interviews to come up with a usable list of potential reinforcers. Following is an example of the lists that were compiled from interviews with one child and his parents:

| Child | Mom | Dad |
|---|---|---|
| Playing outside | Playing | Playing |
| Riding bike | TV | Going with me |
| Fishing with Dad | Riding bike | TV |
| Baseball | Being with Dad | Reading |
| TV | Talking on phone | Riding bike |
| Swimming | Baseball | Minature golf |
| Collecting coins | Cooking | |
| Tennis | Reading | |
| Model airplanes | | |

A glance at these lists shows a fair amount of agreement: Playing, TV, bicycle riding, and doing things with Dad are found on all three lists; baseball and reading appear on two. These are the activities that seem to be especially rewarding for this child. However, keep in mind that these lists relate only to activity rewards. Lists also can be compiled for the other reinforcer categories.

*Feedback.* Success is a powerful motivator. Therefore a potential motivator is feedback, letting the person see signs of success. Feedback includes praise; individual daily records of words written, problems solved, time spent, errors made, tasks completed, points earned, pounds lost, laps run; reports home to parents; work displayed for all to see; movement to higher skill levels in music, karate, mathematics, chess, scouting, and so on. Effective behavior change plans provide abundant feedback on performance and reinforcement for success.

*Sampling.* Perhaps you have bought an item in a supermarket because you tasted a small sample of it. Or perhaps you have watched a long television program because it began with a sample of each of the stories to come. Television producers know that many people need to like only one of the samples to be hooked on the entire program. In like manner, teachers can let so-called unmotivated kids sample a variety of reinforcers until they locate one or two that work. Let the students sample parts of videos, word or mathematical games, and puzzles, for example. Creativity counts. Teachers might try making up word puzzles and verbal games that motivate as well as teach important skills. These, too, can be useful as reinforcers.

*Observation of Friends.* You might get some ideas about motivation and potential reinforcers by observing what the person's close friends and associates enjoy.

*Observation of Misconduct.* Watch what happens after misconduct. Usually there is a payoff for misbehavior. What is the nature of this reinforcer? You may find it worthwhile to identify these payoffs and use them for better ends. A three-year-old child, Nick, liked to jump on the sofa whenever a telephone call to his father interrupted their time together. Because his father attended to the misconduct, Nick was able to regain his father's attention by jumping. The problem was resolved when Nick was given attention for "playing nicely" while his father was on the phone.

## Step 5: Select Teaching Procedures

Several points must be kept in mind as you select and apply strategies for change. First, timing is critical. An effective behavior change plan specifies ways to deliver rewards *immediately* following behavior. Under most circumstances, the sooner a reinforcer follows behavior, the better. This is especially the case when we want to get a new or improved response firmly established. Once a behavior is learned, however, reinforcement can become less frequent and less immediate.

In everyday life, of course, rewards are often delayed for minutes, hours, weeks, and sometimes years. For example, it takes many years of study to become a medical doctor. The chain of events associated with completing the various requirements involves a long, complex series of intellectual, activity, and social reinforcers along the way. While many of these reinforcers are immediate at the time they are received, they are but transitional in terms of the final goal.

Second, consistency is a key to effective change. We must be consistent in the use of incentives and in the overall pursuit of the behavior change plan. Being clear from the outset about the behavior to be changed will help. Thus, for example, if a child is told that he or she can go out to play after completing chores, making playtime available following chores should be a consistent pattern. Communicating this plan is important to maintaining consistency. Keep in mind the importance of getting everyone — spouses, teachers, babysitters — on board with the plan.

Third, feasibility with regard to reinforcers is essential. Be concerned not only with identifying potential rewards but also with their feasibility. Are any too costly? Too controversial? Because social, activity, and tangible rewards are preferred over the use of primary rewards in nonclinical settings, does your plan emphasize these? Can access to reinforcers be regulated? For example, using television as a reinforcer probably will not work if the individual can see as much television as he or she wants away from your program.

Fourth, guard against overuse of any single reinforcer. When a person repeatedly receives a particular reinforcer, that reinforcer may lose its effectiveness. There are ways to avoid this problem. One way is to let the person select from an array, or menu, of five to ten rewards. The menu makes other incentives available when one or more lose their effectiveness. Another way is to control the amount of reinforcement. You will need to determine just how much of a reward (or punisher) to include in your plan. One child in a family may require much more attention than another. This can be a bit tricky. Too much of a good thing may so satisfy the person that future performance suffers, while too little can fail to motivate. Yet another way to avoid overuse of a reinforcer is to let children earn points that can be exchanged for reinforcers later. (I will have more to say about points in the next section.)

## Procedures for Increasing Behavior

What follows is a brief survey of procedures that strengthen or teach new behaviors. While the procedures are discussed separately, there is no reason to select only one. Good plans often employ several procedures.

The first four procedures focus on things that happen before (antecedent to) behavior. Focusing on what comes before behavior can speed learning or short-circuit problem behaviors before they arise. Whenever possible, try one or more of these strategies first.

Do not be surprised if things do not work smoothly in the beginning, but stay with a strategy until you can figure out why it does not work. That information can inform a better choice.

*Instruction.* By "instruction," I mean simple communication, spoken or written directions that tell a person what to do. "Your homework is due tomorrow" and "Keith, come downstairs to dinner" are examples of simple instruction. Most children and youth respond appropriately to this kind of instruction. Some do not respond at first but will after a private, friendly talk requesting cooperation. In resistant cases, we turn to other methods or combine instruction with other approaches.

Possible problems: Instruction sometimes is not useful for very young children, who respond better when they are shown, rather than told, what to do. Communication may be unclear, too complex, or convey a mixed message (Mom says one thing, Dad another).

*Restructuring the Social and Physical Environment.* It is difficult to overstate the importance of making environmental changes to bring about behavior change. The physical and social setting in which behavior occurs has a profound influence on behavior. Compare people's actions at parties versus funerals, or consider how television profoundly and almost immediately changed the behavior of millions of people when it entered homes a half-century ago. More broadly, consider how regional variations dictate what large numbers of people do for a living.

Teachers and parents can bring about behavior change by altering classroom and home settings, including the time and location of activities. One teacher of my acquaintance spent an entire weekend changing various physical features of her classroom to encourage more talk from language-delayed students. Prior to the changes, students had easy access to a variety of reinforcers. After the changes, desired things were placed out of reach (in a closet, in desk drawers, behind barriers). Students then had to chat with the teacher to get previously available items.

Another example involves a teacher working with nine students in a special education resource room. Each day students failed to complete assignments. Nonetheless, they were given daily access to several favored activities (computer time, games, free play). Things changed dramatically when a new rule replaced a previous one: First complete an assignment, then pick an activity. The relationship among situational events (assignments, the new rule), behavior (completing assignments), and the consequences (access to favored activities) is what mattered in this case. Note that a simple change in the situation — the timing of events — had a big effect. Situational change also is at work when students who have difficulty learning assigned material are given supplementary material to study.

In home settings, parents can encourage study by setting up study areas free from distractions. They can spare their toddler a torrent of "No!" by placing fragile objects out of reach. And often they can improve family diets simply by keeping junk foods out of the house. Party hosts also make use of situational changes when they place interesting things around a home that invite comment, as do architects who design homes and buildings to affect human interaction and performance.

Notes and memoranda are aspects of this strategy. If a child forgets to brush her teeth each morning, a self-recording chart taped to the bathroom mirror may help her remember (especially if praise follows). The elderly can reduce frustration associated with taking pills by learning to place their daily assortment in a pill box designed for that purpose. These are relatively simple situational changes, but they can exert a strong influence on human action.

As you think about altering behavior (yours or someone else's), consider changing the physical and social environment. Sometimes modest environmental change is all that is needed. An added advantage is that such change can bring about immediate improvement in behavior without the use of punishment.

Possible problem: Restructuring may not always be possible. For example, funds for special learning materials may not be available or cramped quarters may inhibit useful environmental changes.

*Prompting Desired Behavior.* A child is given a small gift. Because she says nothing in response, her father pats her gently on the shoulder and interjects with "What do you say?" This cues the child to say, "Thank you." This is prompting. A youngster in an earlier example reminded herself to brush her teeth by taping a chart to the bathroom mirror. The chart, which I characterized as part of restructuring the environment, also is a prompt. Any cue that helps someone respond to a new circumstance and to behave in an unaccustomed manner may be considered a kind of prompt.

The use of prompts in teaching often improves instructional effectiveness. Rather than wait for responses to occur, we prompt them so they can be strengthened by reinforcement. Sophisticated prompting can speed up learning.

There are several types of prompts. Guiding an infant's hand to hold and shake a rattle, guiding the hand of a child holding a pencil as he or she forms letters, and guiding a golfer's arms to teach proper form are examples of *physical* prompting. Saying, "Look at me," "Don't forget your lunch money," and "The second President of the United States was John. . . ?" are *verbal* prompts. "This animal says meow" can be a verbal prompt for the response "cat" if, upon seeing a picture of a cat, a child is unable to respond to the question, "What is this animal?" Pictures serve as visual prompts when they accompany new words in a language primer.

Training wheels attached to the rear wheel of a bicycle are *mechanical* prompts, as are crutches if they help someone learn how to walk unaided. Giving directions by pointing illustrates *gestural* prompting (though instruction also may be involved).

A problem arises when we become too dependent on prompts. The child prompted to thank people must at some point learn to be courteous without being prompted. The strategy for withdrawal of prompting is called *fading*, which is the gradual elimination of a prompt. The father can begin fading prompts by, say, eliminating the pat on the shoulder. As his daughter continues to respond appropriately, he can slowly drop the verbal reminder as well, first by lowering his voice, then whispering, and finally merely mouthing the prompt. Training wheels can be faded similarly, by adjusting them upward in a series of small steps until they are eliminated completely. And once the new primer words are learned, the accompanying picture cues can be omitted.

Possible problems: Prompting will not work if the behavior called for is too complex, and inept fading can keep people dependent on prompts.

*Modeling Desired Behavior.* A substantial amount of human behavior is learned in subtle ways by observing what others say and do. The person whose behavior is observed, whether in person or symbolically (in books and on television) is modeling behavior that the observer may imitate either subconsciously or deliberately. And there is strong indication that symbolic models are as influential as live models. Students imitate their textbooks' solutions to problems as well as their teachers'. They imitate the athletic form they see in coaches and players as much from television as at school. They adopt the hairstyles, clothing, and slang they see in the movies as well as among their peers.

And, of course, children imitate behavior they see in their homes. Sensitive and honest parents are likely to raise sensitive, honest children — and vice versa. To teach someone a new behavior, we often prompt an imitative response by performing or demonstrating it. Parents and teachers are familiar with this kind of teaching. A mother shows a child how to sew a basting stitch and then rewards the child's attempts at imitation. When someone learns to pronounce new words, execute a dance step, or program a VCR, they often are instructed to imitate the behavior of their teacher. Like prompting, modeling can speed up learning.

Imitation often occurs in the absence of planned instruction. In fact, children and youth learn many social behaviors informally through imitation. An anti-smoking public service spot on television some years ago powerfully illustrated this point. A father and his young son are shown walking down a country road. After the boy makes a few imitative responses (kicking a pebble after his father does), the two are seen sitting under a tree. The father then lights a cigarette and places the pack between them. As the scene ends, the son is seen picking up the pack and looking at it. The viewer is left with the clear impression that someday the son also will be smoking, just like his dad.

A growing body of evidence shows that people learn both desirable and undesirable behaviors by observing how people who are important to them act. This evidence shows that people generally, and especially children, are likely to imitate others under the following conditions:

The model (parent, teacher, peer, politician) is seen as creditable.

The observer identifies with the model — that is, sees important connections between the model and himself or herself.

The model's behavior is rewarded or, in the case of bad behavior, goes unpunished.

The imitative response itself is rewarded. For example, if a model is seen attracting others with an evocative clothing style, style imitators must be similarly rewarded; otherwise the imitation likely will decline over time.

Possible problems: Imitation does not work if the model behavior is too advanced or too different from the observer's behavior.

*Selective Reinforcement.* To improve or increase a person's performance, positively reinforce its occurrence. This procedure also involves ignoring (extinguishing) undesirable behavior. For example, a young woman and her two-year-old daughter, Anne, came to visit. Anne went immediately to my television set and began tugging at the control knobs. Instead of using physical or verbal punishment, her mother took Anne gently by the hand, led her to a window, and said, "Anne, look at that birdie in the tree." When Anne subsequently engaged in more desirable things (examined a pipe, books), her mother made a point of noticing ("That's a pipe," "See all the books?"). Thus, quite simply and naturally, unacceptable behavior was extinguished and acceptable behavior rewarded with selective reinforcement in the form of attention.

For a teacher the use of response cards during a lecture provides another example of selective reinforcement. Research indicates that lecturing, though widely used at most levels of education, is not especially effective in promoting academic achievement. Why? Most likely because lectures typically emphasize the first component of the ABC model of behavior, while neglecting the second and third. Lecturers typically spend a lot of time presenting information (A) and relatively little providing feedback (C) for student responses (B). When lecturing with response cards, however, a teacher lectures for, say, three to six minutes and then asks a question. Each student responds to the question by writing on a card, holds the card up for inspection, and receives immediate feedback from the teacher. This sequence is repeated many times throughout the lecture. The important point is this: Response-card lectures take seriously each component of the ABC model. Thus they have the potential of promoting higher levels of achievement than do typical lectures.*

Praising or otherwise rewarding a person for good work also involves selective reinforcement — that is, rewarding appropriate but not inappropriate behavior. Examples include: A piano teacher praises a student for playing with feeling, rather than callously; a teacher encourages problem solving instead of rote learning; a parent accepts polite but not rude requests; and a therapist encourages a family to pay more attention to a member's upbeat moods and less attention to somber moods.

Recently, a young wife, concerned about her husband's habit of dropping clothes and other items around the house, started counting items left out of place. Several days later she showed her husband the tally and asked for his help. Then, as he improved, she acknowledged his small improvements, rather than complaining as she had in the past.

Possible problem: Because timing is crucial with selective reinforcement, poor timing can cause problems. For example, slight delays in saying "good" or "yes" can cause a speech therapist to reinforce incorrect, rather than correct, vocal responses.

*Point Systems.* Selective reinforcement also is at work in this strategy. Opportunities to earn points for academic or other performances have been shown to be effective with both individuals and groups, especially when motivation is at a low ebb. Point systems should not be used if simpler strategies (praise, the successful completion of a task) will do. Using points for young people to improve performance has much in common with the use of money as an incentive for adults. Money is exchanged for goods and services. Points, too, are exchanged for other things, called backup reinforcers. And because of their association with backup reinforcers, the points themselves, like money, become reinforcers.

---

*For a fuller discussion of response cards, see Bruno Cipani, *Classroom Management for All Teachers: 11 Effective Plans* (Englewood Cliffs, N.J.: Prentice-Hall, 1998).

A teacher might give points for certain social or academic tasks — for example, giving one or more points for each assignment satisfactorily completed throughout the day. Points have the advantage of offering (for those who need it) a tangible reward immediately after the desired behavior, thus strengthening and motivating behavior. At certain times the earned points can be exchanged for activities or other rewards according to a pre-arranged schedule, say, three points for a certain amount of free time, four points for a visit to another classroom, and so on. Identifying truly motivating backup rewards is essential, otherwise the point system will not work.

Sometimes children are very eager to exchange points and lose motivation if they have to hold onto their points for too long. In these cases, teachers or parents can arrange exchanges to take place, say, at the end of each day and then gradually lengthen the time between exchanges.

Possible problems: The logistics of point systems can be quite demanding. Keeping track of points, nominating effective backup rewards, and managing point exchanges all can be time-consuming.

*Rewarding Step-by-Step Approximations (Shaping).* Perhaps you have played a game in which various small gifts are hidden around someone's home. The object of the game is to search for a gift as others guide you to its location. You are told, "You're getting warm," when moving in the right direction; otherwise you hear, "You're getting cold." Eventually, you find the gift. This little game provides a useful way to look at shaping. It rewards (you're warm) progress small step by small step until a goal is reached.

Teaching a child to act in a *new* way, that is, in a way that is very different for the child, can be accomplished by rewarding small steps toward the new behavior. Teaching a young child to tie his shoe is a case in point. The child can be taught to approach the task a bit at a time. Breaking the task into subtasks, and providing feedback and reinforcement as the child masters each subtask, will work in just about all cases.

Shaping in adults occurs similarly. A woman learning to hit a backhand in tennis can start by gripping the racket correctly. After learning the proper grip, she moves on to her swing, then to her follow through, and so on. After making hundreds of backhand swings and receiving a lot of feedback (from her own body and good coaching) and reinforcement (for good shots), a smooth backhand stroke begins to emerge in a long series of small steps to improvement.

If motivation diminishes or "backsliding" occurs, it may mean that shaping is going too fast. Wise teachers slow down, review, and persist. Change takes time. But persistence will pay off eventually in most cases.

Shaping changes behavior qualitatively as well as quantitatively. Qualitative change refers to altering the form or shape of a response, such as changing a person's golf swing, swimming stroke, French pronunciation, or writing style. Quantitative change emphasizes changes in amount, such as gradually increasing the speed and number of miles jogged or the size and complexity of one's vocabulary.

Rewarding successive approximations is implicated in learning most skills, from simple skills, such as tying one's shoes, to complex ones, such as conducting an orchestra or solving physics problems. Complex skills can take years to master. Skills are learned by way of successive approximations, whether a teacher, the environment, or the activity itself supplies feedback and selective reinforcement.

Shaping is not recommended when instruction, situational changes, prompting, modeling, or selective reinforcement will bring about desired change. When shaping is a sensible course of action, then these other methods may be useful supplemental strategies.

Possible problems: Shaping usually takes time. It has limited value when a "quick fix" is desired. It also may require breaking down a skill into the right series of steps for the learner.

*Contracting.* The use of contracts with children and adults has brought about some remarkable changes in behavior. A contract is a written agreement between two or more people that specifies required behaviors, the responsibilities of those involved, the rewards and privileges available, a record system for determining what rewards and privileges are due, and provisions for negotiation. Bonus arrangements and penalties for contract violations also may be included. Because contracts show the direct relationship of behavior to consequences, they can help settle disputes; the contract can be brought out to find out who promised what.

Three kinds of contracts tend to predominate: School (teacher-student), home (parent-child), and home-school contracts (teachers and parents). The last type holds special promise for several reasons: Powerful rewards often are available in students' homes (access to play, television, the family car, the telephone, special privileges), communication between home and school is fostered, and special treatment is less visible to other students when it takes place in a home setting.

Contracts can be rather simple. For example, Rowena agrees to make her bed, take out the trash, walk the dog, and wash the evening dishes each day. She will earn one point for each of these chores. Twenty-eight points means an option to stay up an extra hour on two nights or five dollars extra allowance. At least 20 points must be earned each week, or Rowena will lose the privilege to watch television on Sunday. If necessary, the contract can be elaborated by making the criteria more explicit, for example, specifying how long the dog is to be walked.

Some contracts must be more complex. The sample contract in the illustration deals with physical aggression. Chris, an aggressive fifth-grader working on changing behavior, receives 20 points at the start of the school day, losing a point each time he acts aggressively. Daily notes home report the points remaining at the end of the day.

Several things about Chris' contract should be noted. First, four contracts preceded the one illustrated. The original contract was in effect for only two days. Because all parties agreed to honor provisions while the contract was in effect, the duration of

```
                              Contract

For Week Beginning _____ Ending _____

Item or Activity            Cost in Points
Ice Cream                         2
TV (each half hour)               2
Twenty-five cents                 2
Cooking with Mom                  5
Out to play after school         10
Putt-Putt golf with Dad          15
Fishing with Dad                 15
Movie with family                15

              Signed  _____
                      (Dad)

                      _____
                      (Mom)

                      _____
                      (Chris)

Bonus:        20 points from school = 5 pts; 18 = 3; 16 = 2
Negotiation:  At end of contract period
Penalties:    Lose point for each physical contact such as hit-
              ting, grabbing, shoving, chasing. Above
              items/activities available only with points.
```

the initial contracts was kept short (2 or 3 days each). Problems that arose were noted and considered in subsequent contract negotiations.

Second, initial contracts listed more items and activities than those shown here (Chris did not select several of the backup rewards originally identified; these were dropped from subsequent contracts).

Third, to keep contracts honest, most items and activities were qualified. For example, "Going fishing with Dad" was qualified parenthetically with "at mutually agreeable times."

Fourth, the most desirable or hard-to-arrange rewards cost more points.

# Point Record

For Week Beginning _____ Ending _____

| Days | Points from school | Out to Play | Putt-Putt with Dad | 25 Cents | TV | Ice Cream | Movie with family | Cooking with Mom | Fishing with Dad | Points remaining for Day |
|------|------|------|------|------|------|------|------|------|------|------|
| Example Oct. 1 | 20 | 10 | | 4 | | | | | | 6 |
| | | | | | | | | | | |
| | | | | | | | | | | |
| | | | | | | | | | | |
| | | | | | | | | | | |
| | | | | | | | | | | |
| | | | | | | | | | | |
| | | | | | | | | | | |

Total Points Remaining

Contracts of some complexity will require their own point records to keep track of points earned or lost. The sample point record illustrates the first day of a new contract, October 1. This point record was kept at home by Chris and his parents. Chris began with 20 points, having lost none to aggressive behavior at school, and "spent" 10 points to go out to play after school and 4 points to get 50¢ (to spend on a soda), leaving a balance of 6 points.

Whenever possible, contracts should be negotiated. All parties should view the contract as fair and enter into it with realistic intentions of carrying it out. Try to state the contract in positive terms, using more do's than don'ts. Keep the expectations realistic. For example, Chris was charged 15 points to go fishing with his father. Fortunately, he spent a good deal of time with his father apart from contract arrangements. If that were not the case, the relatively high point requirement to spend time with his father would have been suspect. Also, it is a good idea to date and sign contracts. Along with negotiation, this "formal" procedure can boost participants' commitment.

Possible problems: Basic elements may be missing from the contract, which may cause confusion or bad feelings. Parties may pledge cooperation but not follow through. All parties may not be fully informed about their responsibilities. Record keeping may be taxing or slipshod.

## Procedures for Decreasing Behavior

The procedures to weaken or eliminate behavior discussed in this section are classified into five levels in order of preference, though unusual circumstances may call for a different order. The procedures listed illustrate only some of the promising strategies available at each level. Some of the terms may be unfamiliar, but I will define them as we go along. When selecting strategies, start with Level 1 and, if necessary, work your way to Level 5.

Level 1. Instruction; restructure the social and physical environment.

Level 2. Reward the absence of the behavior; reward incompatible behavior; reward lower rates of the behavior.

Level 3. Ignore it.

Level 4. Response cost; time-out (non-exclusionary); time-out (exclusionary).

Level 5. Strong reprimanding; overcorrection; practicing inappropriate behavior; expending effort; physical restraint; spanking.

At Level 1 the focus is on quick solutions. These are the approaches you should emphasize. At Level 2 the use of reinforcement predominates. These, too, are highly recommended. Level 3 makes use of extinction, while the Level 4 procedures relate to negative punishment. Level 5 includes the last-resort, positive punishment procedures that require one to ask, Have I seriously tried the strategies in the first four levels? If the answer is "no," then refrain from using Level 5 strategies. These levels also are relevant when considering least restrictive environments for learning.

*Level 1*

*Instruction*, as in the section on strengthening behavior, is concerned with simple spoken or written requests, directions, warnings, and so on, but this time the intent is to weaken behavior. Parents and teachers who are characteristically indecisive or inconsistent in making requests — sometimes they mean what they say, sometimes they don't — create problems for themselves. Unless exposed to inconsistency, most kids will respond most of the time when asked to stop doing something. But, as we all know, something else may be needed.

Possible problems: The more the teacher said to sit down, the more students got out of their seats. This is the conclusion of a well-known study* that I cite to emphasize the point that attention can be a very powerful reinforcer, even when it is meant to be negative. Keep the following principle in mind when using

*C. Madsen et al., "An Analysis of the Reinforcing Functions of 'Sit Down' Commands," in *Readings in Educational Psychology*, edited by R. Parker (Boston: Allyn & Bacon, 1968), pp. 265-278.

instruction to weaken behavior: We risk energizing misconduct when we call attention to it.

*Restructure the Social and Physical Environment.* Modifying the physical and social environment is a powerful way to weaken behavior, as well as to strengthen it. Everyone has seen behavior decrease in response to an environmental change. For instance, when a room is too cold, adjusting the thermostat may reduce complaints or keep people from leaving. Fast-food restaurants make use of environmental control when they use uncomfortable furniture to discourage loitering.

Teachers and parents also make situational changes to reduce behavior. When two students cannot keep from talking, seating them apart often solves the problem. And there is evidence that cleaning up immediately after a school is vandalized discourages additional incidents. In addition, some schools have restocked or removed vending machines to reduce the consumption of junk food during school hours.

Making situational changes also can reduce boredom. One possibility is to introduce variety or novelty. Another possibility is to change the time of an event. One teacher, finding her students in the doldrums after lunch each day, moved a popular morning activity (science) to the after-lunch period with great success.

Possible problems: Restructuring a situation may not be possible, or it may take too much time to accomplish.

*Level 2*

*Reward the Absence of Behavior.* The technical name for this strategy is "differential reinforcement of other behavior" (DRO for short). This is a relatively simple procedure in which any acceptable behavior is reinforced at the end of a specified period of time provided that an undesirable behavior is *absent* during the time period. For example, Jamie is hooked on television, watching it after school about five hours each day. Concerned that television predominately rewards "watching" and nurtures inactivity, his mother decides to cut back the amount of viewing by dividing after school hours into half-hour segments and rewarding any acceptable behavior (reading, playing, talking, cooking) whenever Jamie refrains from watching television for an entire segment. The length of segments is to be increased gradually until Jamie watches no more than 90 minutes a day.

Note that Jamie's mother began at a level (30 minutes) considerably lower than the initial level of watching (5 hours). This is characteristic of good behavior change plans: Setting subgoals so that desirable behavior is both bound to occur and rewarded in a series of small steps leading to improvement. A potential outcome of this strategy is that Jamie will learn to like other things that will serve him well in life (such as playing the guitar, working crossword puzzles, skiing, reading, and so on).

This technique can be used to reduce many behaviors, such as cussing, teasing, being late, noncompliance, whining, staring into space, talking, clowning, arguing, tattling, fighting with little sister, and wandering.

Possible problem: When an undesirable behavior is absent throughout a time segment, be careful not to reward some other undesirable behavior that occurs at the end of the segment. In such cases, simply withhold rewards and start a new segment.

*Reward Incompatible Behavior.* The technical name for this is "differential reinforcement of incompatible behavior" (DRI for short). When behaviors are incompatible, they cannot take place at the same time. Being in one's seat and wandering around the classroom are incompatible. But, as every teacher knows, being in one's seat and whispering are not incompatible. Rewarding incompatible behavior is a more precise strategy than rewarding the absence of behavior. The procedure is designed to strengthen behavior that is contrary to undesirable behavior, thus eliminating the undesirable behavior.

Suppose a student frequently is out of her seat or off-task, takes things that do not belong to her, and leaves the classroom without permission. Instead of confronting all four behaviors (a rough rule is to concentrate on one or two), the teacher might begin by rewarding in-seat and on-task activities. Note that the other problem behaviors cannot be occurring when the student is in her seat and working on her assignments.

A mother who prevents thumb sucking by keeping her daughter's hands busy with rewarding things to do also is using this technique. If she were to combine this technique with reinforcement for the absence of thumb sucking, the chances of eliminating thumb sucking would be even greater.

Possible problem: Finding incompatible behaviors that are beneficial, rather than trivial, may be difficult.

*Reward Lower Rates of the Behavior.* The technical name for this is "differential reinforcement of a low rate of behavior" (DRL). Sometimes this strategy amounts to little more than rewarding the absence of behavior. However, its focus is on gradually reducing, rather than eliminating, behavior. Assume a young adolescent consumes too many daily calories — averaging 4,200 rather than a desirable 1,700. Over a number of weeks, her mother arranges effective rewards to follow daily consumption of 3,800 calories, then 3,500, then 3,200, and so on, until the goal of 1,700 is reached. A teacher might use this technique to gradually reduce the number of times a student needlessly asks for help or delays getting down to work.

Possible problem: Judging how much to reduce behavior may be difficult. If someone monopolizes classroom discussions, for example, just how much participation is appropriate for the student?

*Level 3*

*Ignore Inappropriate Behavior.* Ignoring a previously rewarded behavior (extinction) is a Level 3 procedure. Ignoring behavior means not attending to it in any way, not commenting on it, and not looking in its direction.

The following illustrates extinction in everyday life: An eleven-year-old boy developed a habit of "nervous eye blinking." His mother and younger sister talked a lot about it in his presence. After a doctor ruled out any physical problem, both mother and sister completely ignored the blinking. It was gone in a few weeks.

Remember: We risk energizing behavior when we call attention to it. In fact, some theorists believe that many problem behaviors result from some sort of misplaced attention (approval, recognition). Clowning in class, gossiping, complaining, throwing tantrums, tattling, and offensive language are cases in point. Completely ignoring these behaviors should eliminate them. But, of course, that often is easier said than done.

Possible problems: You may not be able to ignore behavior if others present do not also ignore it or if the person is harming himself or others. Also, extinction tends to be a rather slow process, behavior may get worse before it gets better, and retaliatory aggression is not unusual. It is hard to maintain a consistent approach under these conditions.

## Level 4

*Response Cost.* Response cost is a procedure whereby a reward or privilege is taken away when misconduct occurs. Fining someone for an infraction or telling quarreling children that they can not go to a promised movie are response cost procedures designed to reduce infractions and quarreling in the future. Response cost ushers us into the realm of (negative) punishment. If punishment is to be used, restrict it to response cost, if possible.

Response cost is fairly easy to apply. And there often is an opportunity to reinstate a lost privilege once the person is back on track. When using response cost, consider having the person forfeit small amounts of the privilege. Five minutes lost from recess for each offense probably is preferable to taking away recess entirely. You always can deduct more time (10 or 15 minutes) if you need to. Also, it is not unusual to combine response cost with another approach, say, a point system of reinforcement. If a student is earning points for other things, some of the points might be forfeited after engaging in undesirable behavior. The student should be informed beforehand if he is to lose points he has earned.

Possible problems: Expect some complaining about the loss of privileges. Do not forget to reward good behavior when punishment is used (loss of a privilege for swearing *and* praise for acceptable talk). Consistency is a must: Give one warning and follow through, otherwise response cost will become little more than an idle threat.

*Time-out (Non-Exclusionary).* Time-out means time away from a reinforcing setting for a specified period each time misconduct occurs — usually 5 to 10 minutes for children five and older, only about one minute for each year of life for younger children. Time-out is more complex than response cost in that *the person* is not allowed access to a variety of reinforcers (playing, talking, moving about, hearing a story). In response cost, *a reinforcer* is removed after a particular act.

In non-exclusionary time-out, the person remains in the room but is in some way separated from others. For example, a child may be required to sit in a part of the room away from the rest of the children each time she grabs a toy from someone. She may even sit behind a partition that shields her from others. At the elementary school level, a convenient procedure is worthy of note. It involves a time-out badge or a participation card placed near each child's work area. The children have access to all rewards normally available while wearing the badge or displaying the card. When undesirable behavior occurs, the child surrenders her badge or card for a brief time during which she is restricted from normal activities. When time-out is over, the badge or card is returned.*

Possible problems: Time-out will not work unless the person finds the unrestricted setting rewarding in the first place. Because the child may get out of the time-out area repeatedly, it may be necessary to remain in the time-out area — or gently hold the child in a chair — until the child catches on. On such occasions, the teacher or parent should refrain from interacting with the child as much as possible. Overusing time-out is another problem.

---

*An early work on this strategy is R.M. Foxx and S.T. Shapiro, "The Timeout Ribbon: A Non-Exclusionary Timeout Procedure," *Journal of Applied Behavior Analysis* 11 (Spring 1978): 125-36.

*Time-out (Exclusionary).* This is similar to non-exclusionary time-out except that the person is sent to an area in another room, an area that is well-lighted, well-ventilated, and safe, but dull. The idea behind both time-out procedures is that the person goes from a rewarding setting to one that is unrewarding. This should not be confused with putting someone in a frightening place, such as a closet, which is inhumane and inappropriate. Time-out is a move to boredom, not to fright or excessive deprivation.

When implementing a time-out procedure, there are several points to keep in mind:

Tell the person privately how time-out will work. If you think it will help, role-play important aspects of the procedure. Let the person know what will happen if she refuses time-out.

Give one warning: "Sarah, if you do that again, it's time-out."

If a time-out is warranted, lead the child to the time-out area calmly and silently. Ignore complaints. If you do talk, remain impersonal and stay with facts, such as, "You can't throw things in here."

If the child is noisy in time-out, ignore her.

The child may leave time-out when the time is up, providing that she has acted appropriately (not yelling, complaining) for 15 to 30 seconds prior to release. If not, time-out should continue for another minute before termination, again provided the behavior is acceptable for the last 15 to 30 seconds of the added minute. (Generally, total time-out should not exceed 30 minutes.) Consider adding a response cost if the extra minutes do not work.

When the child returns to the original setting, quickly catch her being good and acknowledge it in some way to reinforce appropriate behavior.

Possible problems: Some educators and parents oppose exclusionary time-out on humanitarian grounds, often because they view it as unwarranted deprivation. Some students will refuse time-out and must be dealt with in other ways.

*Level 5*

*Strong Reprimanding.* Strong reprimands — scolding, such as, "Stop it!" and "Clean up your language, Now!" — are a familiar way to stop behavior. Unlike instruction, rules, and directions, reprimands are more demanding and come after, rather than before, an act. Because strong reprimands amount to positive punishment and the line between them and verbal abuse is thin, it makes sense to be cautious in one's choice of words. Whenever possible, reprimands should:

- focus on a specific behavior, not personal attributes;
- specify what needs to be changed; and
- be delivered firmly but calmly.

Hollering "Stop it!" probably will work less effectively than a firm, "Stop throwing that ball in here. You can throw it outdoors later."

Possible problems: Angry reprimands may lead to verbal abuse and alienation. Scolding without backup punishment may cause more misconduct if one ends up merely calling attention to misconduct.

*Overcorrection.* This method has two elements. First, the person is required to correct and improve a situation that was disturbed by his or her misconduct. For example, if a teenage boy repeatedly wears his brother's clothes without permission, he might be required to wash and iron both what he has worn (correction) and additional items from his brother's wardrobe (overcorrection).

Second, repeated practice may be required. That is, the person is to repeatedly practice an *appropriate* related behavior to the point of aversion. In the case of the teenager, he might be required to repeatedly apologize to family members or repeatedly request permission, or both. Because overcorrection is a positive punishment procedure, the person should not be rewarded in any way as he engages in one or both forms of the procedure.

In a school setting, overcorrection might be considered for very difficult cases. Suppose a student regularly keeps a messy work area (locker room space, seat on the school bus). He might be required to clean up the area and several additional areas (overcorrection). If that fails to change the behavior, he might be required to repeatedly arrange objects (such as books, kitchen items, other materials) in a neat and orderly way (appropriate practice).

Overcorrection has been helpful with mentally disabled children and adults, autistic children, and the emotionally disabled. One or both forms of overcorrection have been used to reduce aggression and other disruptive behaviors, toilet accidents, shouting, swearing, tantrums, self-injurious behavior, and more.

Possible problems: Overcorrection often requires close supervision, and some individuals will refuse to comply. In many situations it may be necessary to gain official approval from supervising authorities before using this strategy.

*Practicing Inappropriate Behavior.* Unlike overcorrection, where one practices an appropriate behavior, this strategy calls for practicing an incorrect or unwanted behavior to the point of fatigue or aversion. One mother stopped her daughters from jumping on their beds by requiring them to do so well beyond the point of enjoyment. In school settings, some behaviors — swearing, throwing things — might be similarly reduced, but away from the view of other students.

Possible problems: Like overcorrection, this strategy demands close supervision; and some individuals will refuse to cooperate. Obviously, some inappropriate behaviors — aggression, smoking — should not be practiced.

*Expending Effort.* This procedure requires physical activity after each act of misconduct. The person might be required, say, to sit on the floor and stand up several times (10, 20, 30 times) in quick succession. However, only moderate measures should be used — that is, the person should be able to engage in the physical activity with little or no strain.

Possible problems: The person may not cooperate or be able to comply. Proper authorization may be needed before using this strategy.

*Physical Restraint.* On rare occasions, to prevent serious injury to self, physical harm to others, or destruction of property, physical restraint may be necessary. Restraint may require placing the misbehaving individual on the floor while preventing movement of his or her limbs and torso. The individual is released when he or she calms down. However, physical restraint can be risky and should be used only in extreme circumstances. Stay alert to the possibility that physical contact and attention to aggressive acts might actually increase them.

Possible problems: Physical restraint may require the cooperative efforts of several individuals. It must be clearly authorized by supervisors and must be used consistent with policy. Planning and simulated practice of the restraint techniques is a must.

*Spanking.* Spanking (or any form of corporal punishment) is not recommended, though this behavior change strategy is still sanctioned in some states and local school districts. A statement by the American Academy of Pediatrics provides helpful guidance on this matter.*

## Summary Guidelines

You may find the following general guidelines useful when taking disciplinary action.

Be firm, but stay calm (use a low, steady voice).

Respond to the infraction as soon as possible.

Be consistent. Say what you mean, and mean what you say. Do not threaten and then not follow through (this *teaches* kids to ignore requests).

Do not say how the misbehavior makes you feel ("You're driving me crazy"). Later, of course, sharing thoughts and feelings may be helpful.

Do not overreact. Usually, small rewards and punishers, when part of a good plan, will work fine.

Try to reward an alternative behavior whenever punishment is used. For example, if little Blakey is reprimanded for rough play, make a point of recognizing cooperative play.

---

*American Academy of Pediatrics, "Guidance for Effective Discipline," *Pediatrics* 101 (April 1998): 723-28.

Above all, direct criticism at the child's actions, not at the child personally. Overgeneralized statements, such as "What's wrong with you?" and "Can't you do anything right?" do not get at specific action and should be avoided.

## Step 6: Rehearse Key Elements

Readers who have been active in theater understand the importance of dress rehearsals in preparing for opening night. Role-playing key elements of a behavior change plan can produce similar benefits. If a student with whom you are working does not understand what you mean by "argumentative," consider demonstrating what you mean, not for only him to see, but for other participants in the plan as well. Similarly, consider rehearsing other key parts of your plan, such as a time-out procedure, counting and record keeping, modeling, and the use of feedback and reinforcement. Good rehearsals can teach people a lot in a very short period of time

## Step 7: Implement the Plan

As you put the plan in motion, let everyone involved know how to contact you should things not run smoothly. The checklist on page 82 can help you determine whether things are in place at this juncture. Consider each item carefully.

## Step 8: Monitor Results

This step involves trouble-shooting and adjustment, observing the target behavior using the same methods as in Step 2. Comparing information from this phase with information from Step 2 also will help you judge the behavior change plan's effectiveness.

Often one finds it necessary to change one's own behavior in response to how the person responds to the plan. Should you find progress at a standstill, discuss the situation with the participants. Has the delivery of rewards been delayed? Have key people been left out of negotiations? Are the standards too high or too low? Is

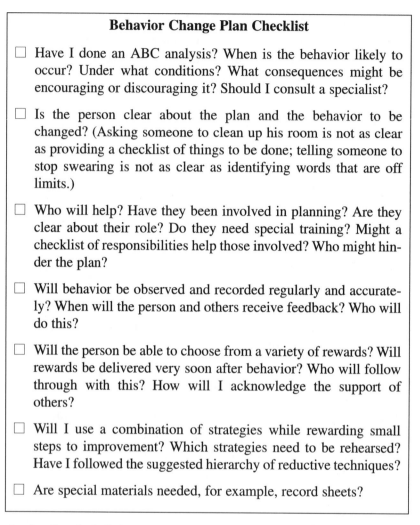

**Behavior Change Plan Checklist**

☐ Have I done an ABC analysis? When is the behavior likely to occur? Under what conditions? What consequences might be encouraging or discouraging it? Should I consult a specialist?

☐ Is the person clear about the plan and the behavior to be changed? (Asking someone to clean up his room is not as clear as providing a checklist of things to be done; telling someone to stop swearing is not as clear as identifying words that are off limits.)

☐ Who will help? Have they been involved in planning? Are they clear about their role? Do they need special training? Might a checklist of responsibilities help those involved? Who might hinder the plan?

☐ Will behavior be observed and recorded regularly and accurately? When will the person and others receive feedback? Who will do this?

☐ Will the person be able to choose from a variety of rewards? Will rewards be delivered very soon after behavior? Who will follow through with this? How will I acknowledge the support of others?

☐ Will I use a combination of strategies while rewarding small steps to improvement? Which strategies need to be rehearsed? Have I followed the suggested hierarchy of reductive techniques?

☐ Are special materials needed, for example, record sheets?

the feedback deficient? Are the procedures inconsistent? And so on. You may even want to consult relevant literature to see how others have dealt with any problem you encounter. But try not to change the plan until you have a fair idea of what's wrong.

In other words, be willing to make adjustments in your behavior change plan, but try not to be impatient. It may take several days or even weeks for a plan to work. And it is not unusual for behavior to get worse before it gets better. The important thing is to collect daily information to help you decide what to do next, make adjustments as needed, and continue monitoring.

## Step 9: Maintain and Generalize Gains

Once behavior has changed for the better, attention shifts to whether the person will retain and use the newly acquired behavior in other appropriate locations or situations (generalization). "Generalization" can be viewed as "transfer of learning." This is an essential element of any form of teaching. And this step, unfortunately, is when many otherwise effective behavior change plans break down.

It can be disheartening to see a child return to his possessive ways after being taught to share his toys, or to see that sharing takes place only when his teacher or parent is around. Following are some ways to promote retention and generalization of a behavior change:

*Practice and review.* Many things are forgotten and unavailable for use because they were not learned well in the first place. The remedy is practice and periodic review.

*Pay attention to settings.* Sometimes we teach someone to behave in a setting so unlike other settings that it makes generalization unlikely. For example, a teacher who teaches a child to share by frequently praising his efforts may be working at cross-purposes with the child's parents, who allow possessiveness and never praise sharing at home. A parental conference and cooperative plan might help remedy the situation.

The timing of reinforcement provides another example of how dissimilar settings can discourage generalization. When teaching a new behavior, we often provide continuous reinforcement. But reinforcement in the real world tends to be intermittent, not continuous. The solution is to reward new behavior intermittently, once it is well established.

*Teach flexibly.* Rigid teaching and rote learning generally interfere with retention and generalization. Using a variety of teaching methods can promote flexibility in learners. For example, suppose you are using modeling and role play to teach someone to initiate conversations. Ask the person to role play not only with you, but also with others. Vary the theme of each role play. Such flexibility is likely to encourage retention and generalization beyond the teaching setting.

*Encourage application.* Imagine a teacher who, after identifying various techniques of propaganda (negative labeling, repetitive messages, bandwagon appeals), asks students to memorize definitions and examples. Now imagine another teacher who, after discussing propaganda techniques in class, asks students to locate their own examples on television, in song lyrics, and so on. All else being equal, the second teacher — because learning has been related to daily life and extended to situations outside the classroom — has done more to encourage retention and generalization than the first teacher. Similarly, a student who has learned to start conversations in school might be asked to try his or her new skills at home with parents, neighbors, community leaders, and others.

*Fade artificial or unnatural strategies.* Using artificial techniques to change behavior — such as the light switch in the case of the kindergarten teacher I mentioned earlier — can hinder generalization. Gradually eliminate such techniques, so that the newly acquired behavior will appear under more normal circumstances.

I have devoted this long chapter to describing a general plan of action and some specific strategies for changing behavior. Next, the final chapter of this book will show how an effective behavior plan works in practice.

# Chapter Six

# The Plan in Practice

In this last chapter I present three cases that exemplify the nine-step process that I have described. Each case is shown in outline form with an introductory statement to set the stage.

## Case 1: Reducing Aggression, A Case of Too Much Behavior

Communication between home and school was strained when this consultation began. The subject, Chris, was a fifth-grade male with a reputation as a fighter. Fortunately, his aggression was fairly mild, causing more anxiety and annoyance than physical pain. The problem initially was denied by both parents. But their view changed markedly when they saw a simple baseline graph of the problem. (You may recall that I discussed this type of graph in Step 2 in the previous chapter.) Their change in outlook played a key role in the outcome of this case. Their reaction to the data shows how merely collecting and displaying information can help change behavior.

*Step 1: Define behavior.*
   Aggression included hitting with open or closed hands, grabbing, shoving, and chasing.
*Step 2: Estimate its amount.*
   Frequency recording was used. The baseline averaged about 40 daily incidents during gym and lunch period (no aggression in classroom or on playground).

*Step 3: Set attainable goals.*

Reduce aggression in two settings to near zero level.

*Step 4: Identify potential reinforcers.*

Several effective rewards were identified, including spending time with Dad.

*Step 5: Select teaching procedures.*

Graphed data shown to participants.

Praise and recognition given for progress.

Response cost used — loss of point for each aggressive act from 20 points given daily.

Used home-school contract; points remaining from school exchanged for backup rewards at home.

*Step 6: Rehearse key elements.*

Rehearsal was done in school and at home.

*Step 7: Implement the plan.*

The number of acts initially increased.

*Step 8: Monitor results.*

Heavy monitoring was used during the first week. An uneven reduction occurred, finally reducing aggressive acts to an average of three a week by the end of a three-month period.

*Step 9: Maintain and generalize gains.*

The point system was faded; and after 2 months, bonus points were earned when Chris counted his own behavior. Complete self-control was achieved toward the end of case. Social attention for absence of fighting was continued.

## Case 2: Increasing Motivation, A Case of Too Little Behavior

The subject was a 16-year-old female, Kay, described as academically unmotivated. Her parents were concerned about her long-standing lack of interest in school and her failure to complete homework assignments. Kay scored high average on an individual intelligence test and was enrolled in a college preparatory curriculum, but the family had difficulty functioning as a cohesive unit. This case is an example of a plan that was inconsistently applied and therefore only moderately successful.

*Step 1: Define behavior.*

The problem was failure to complete homework.

*Step 2: Estimate amount.*

Product recording was used to show that only about 20% of assignments were completed.

*Step 3: Set attainable goals.*

The goal was to increase homework completion to 100% in a series of steps, with the expectation that Kay's grades would improve.

*Step 4: Identify potential reinforcers.*

Reinforcers were identified as extra allowance money and access to the telephone, television, and family car.

*Step 5: Select teaching procedures.*

The physical environment for studying was changed. For example, the TV and phone were removed from the study area.

Assignments were broken down into smaller units.

Completion of units was rewarded with minutes on the phone, TV time, or car mileage. Extra allowance was used as a bonus.

Parents were to check on homework completion.

*Step 6: Rehearse key elements.*

Procedures were rehearsed with Kay and her parents, including how homework would be assessed.

*Step 7: Implement the plan.*

All parties were initially enthusiastic, but the plan was administered inconsistently.

*Step 8: Monitor results.*

Inconsistency led to many adjustments in procedures. Assignment completion did rise to nearly 70%, and grades rose from D to C average over the course of the year.

*Step 9: Maintain and generalize gains.*

Fading was not feasible; and the plan, with altered procedures, was carried into the next year. This illustrates the problem of inconsistency. Had the original plan been consistently implemented, Kay might have changed her behavior enough to maintain a more successful pattern on her own.

## Case 3: Group Management, A Case of an Unruly Class

This case involved 23 fourth-grade students who "refused to get down to work," in the words of their teacher. The teacher had been an elementary school teacher for more than 20 years at the time of the case. The classroom was loosely structured; and though the teacher's manner was amiable, he was easily distracted by the antics of the students. This case illustrates how attending to structure and management principles can bring about useful change.

*Step 1: Define behavior.*
Behavior to be changed was being out of seat, facing away from the teacher, or frequent talk.

*Step 2: Estimate amount.*
Time sampling for two hours daily showed that about two-thirds of the class engaged in inappropriate behavior during much of the class time.

*Step 3: Set attainable goals.*
The goal was to increase appropriate behavior: in seat, facing teacher, on task, following directives.

*Step 4: Identify potential reinforcers.*
A reinforcement menu was developed by interviewing class leaders, then the entire class voted on the menu items.

*Step 5: Select teaching procedures.*
The graphed data were shown to the class.
Praise and recognition were given for appropriate behavior. Inappropriate acts were ignored for the most part, something the teacher had difficulty doing.
Students earned points if everyone was engaged in appropriate behavior when a kitchen timer rang on a variable interval schedule.
Points could be exchanged for menu items.

*Step 6: Rehearse key elements.*
Procedures were rehearsed with the entire class, and the support of the class leaders was enlisted.

*Step 7: Implement the plan.*

The plan worked well from the beginning. The inclusion of class leaders was instrumental.

*Step 8: Monitor results.*

Appropriate behaviors began to dominate early on.

*Step 9: Maintain and generalize gains.*

Praise continued; the use of the kitchen timer was faded and replaced by the teacher's "Okay," delivered at variable intervals. Points were faded by the end of the year.

## A Final Word

A book such as this one may leave the impression that people are to be seen as mere objects to be manipulated in some dispassionate way. That is a false impression. The plan described here is not simply about teaching discrete tasks and skills. It is about helping people, whether students or adults, to change in the context of a relationship in which they feel accepted and secure. This requirement can be obscured by the shorthand manner in which I have outlined the preceding cases. In fact, the relationship between the consultant and the others involved in these cases was sensitive and friendly.

Self-control, or self-discipline, is the real goal of all behavior change. A case outlined in Chapter 6 illustrates this point: Chris, an aggressive fifth-grader, lost a point each time he got into a scuffle. Initially other people kept track of his aggression. But by the end of the case he was counting and controlling his own behavior without outside assistance. In short, though the approach outlined in these pages is a promising one for changing behavior, it is useful only insofar as it helps people increase their ability to direct the course of their own life experiences.

In the Foreword to the second edition of John Goodlad's *What Schools Are For* (Phi Delta Kappa Educational Foundation, 1994), esteemed educator Ralph W. Tyler calls attention to the common purpose of schools: The education of children and youth to become informed, responsible citizens. He continues:

The school can help individual students to clarify their aspirations, develop a plan for the step-by-step attainment of those aspirations, monitor their progress, and try to understand and alleviate the problems they encounter. (pp. vii-viii)

Tyler's interest in the self-discipline of individuals, worthy goals, step-by-step planning, monitoring, and problem solving is the stuff about which this book also is concerned. These processes are at the heart of behavior change. They are as important in the home — and in our adult lives — as they are in the school.

# About the Author

Frank J. Sparzo is a professor of psychology in the Department of Educational Psychology at Ball State University. He specializes in applied behavior analysis, learning, and psychoeducational measurement and evaluation. Prior to joining the faculty at Ball State, Sparzo held other teaching positions in psychology and had been a dean of students. His Ph.D. is from Johns Hopkins University.

Sparzo is the author of two titles in Phi Delta Kappa's fastback series, 221 *Changing Behavior: A Practical Guide for Teachers and Parents* and 311 *Preparing Better Teacher-Made Tests*. He also has published articles and book chapters in the areas of learning and educational measurement. His most recent publication attempts to identify critical problems that are likely to deeply affect education in the 21st century and beyond.

Since 1985, Sparzo has been a lecturer in the Phi Delta Kappa Educational Foundation's Author Seminar-Lecture Program. He has presented workshops and lectured in nearly 40 states and abroad. Sparzo also consults with parents and teachers and is involved in community service projects.